Stories that Changed the World

Mary Kay Jennings

A ShortWorks Humanities Mini Text Series
Volume 1

Stories that Changed the World

— An Imprint of —

A Project of Urbandale Studios Inc.
Freiburg, Germany | Los Angeles, USA

www.shortworks.co

ISBN: 1514225786
ISBN-13: 978-1514225783

Introduction

The idea of the "story" often conjures up the kinds of tales we encountered as children, ones that swept us away to different times and places, took us on adventures we could never have experienced under the protection of our families. And this may well illustrate the power of the story at its most fundamental level—to transport us out of ourselves, offer us experiences that we may otherwise never have, and allow us to empathize with the characters that have them.

Still, the act of storytelling is more complicated than it first appears. For example, in studying *the humanities*, we will encounter "stories" in many forms: in the visual arts (painting, sculpture, ornamentation), the performing arts (drama and dance), music, literature (stories both oral and written), religion, philosophy, and history. All fall under the umbrella term, *the humanities*, and all have a "story" to tell. Storytelling may be the most powerful attribute we humans possess. The ability to tell stories may be responsible for our domination of the planet Earth and our capacity to learn and pass on information from one generation to another; it may even hold the key to our survival as a species. In essence, our ability to tell stories may have been what made us "human" in the first place and what has enabled us to participate in a story told on the grandest scale: The Human Story.

The Human Story began perhaps six million years ago before our species even evolved into the creatures we are today. Since then, our storytelling ability has played a powerful role in the development of our world civilizations, in our tragedies, and in our successes. It has empowered us to build great monuments like the pyramids in Egypt over 4000 years ago and space contraptions that allowed us to walk on the moon. But it has also enabled us to manufacture bombs—the atomic bomb and its cousin, the hydrogen bomb—that could annihilate mankind if put in the wrong hands. Storytelling carries with it tremendous responsibilities along with potential dangers if misused. In the wrong hands of greedy leaders, corporations, or technocrats, we could see our freedoms, our independent thought processes, and perhaps our continued ability to function as human beings disappear.

Which stories will we choose to tell in this century and beyond? Which stories will we choose to believe? What will be the consequences of our choices? Recognizing that stories can empower or corrupt, these are some of the questions we will entertain in our study of *Stories that Changed the World*. Unless we acknowledge the importance of storytelling, recognize the power it can exert on us as human beings, and assess the motives behind the stories we tell and are told, we become storytelling's victims, our brains given over to men or machines that will do our thinking for us.

Part I: Becoming Human

The following is a "story" of how our species became human. It is derived from recent studies by scientists who investigate how neurons and electrical impulses in our brains connect to form patterns. This "story" is exclusively mine though I will give credit to the scientists who have contributed evidence used to formulate this story.

Stories are hardwired. First, we seem "hardwired" to tell stories. Evolutionary biologists have hypothesized this idea. They propose that we humans are bombarded with so much sensory information coming into our brains via our senses (seeing, smelling, touching, tasting, feeling) that we can process only a fragment of it. The initial act of storytelling (telling a story to ourselves) enables us to "connect the dots" and makes the world and our place in it more coherent. According to Michael Gazzaniga, neuroscientist and author of *Cognitive Science: The Biology of the Mind* (2014), *coherence* in the story we tell is more important than its truth because coherence produces a pattern and provides a structure for our experience; it gives our story a beginning, a middle, and an end. Thus, our brains assemble and "confabulate" a narrative to help us make sense of our experience. ("Confabulate"—tell a story—is a word that both Gazzaniga and another famous scientist, Edward O. Wilson use to explain the process by which our brains transform raw sensory data into useful patterns.)

Gazzaniga explains this process in some detail in his textbook. Having made numerous studies of the brain's right and left hemispheres, he points out the different function of each sphere. The right hemisphere, he says, has a narrow awareness of the world and acts as a monitor, gathering information in a mostly unconscious way and storing it in millions of microscopic physical systems. The left hemisphere acts as the "Interpreter" (Gazzaniga's term), gathering "thousands of bits of information from all over the cortex," organizing them into a cause-effect scenario, a " 'makes-sense' narrative, our personal story" (620). The left hemisphere creates the narrative, rationalizes irrational behavior, forms beliefs, and creates goals. The left hemisphere gathers information, organizes it into a coherent story within our environment, and creates the narrative of our lives. Also, according to Gazzaniga our minds often invent events that never happened and people who don't exist just to "hold the narrative together."

In addition, Jason Gots, an economist and neuroscience researcher, explains in an article entitled "Your Storytelling Brain," that storytelling is "essential to our survival" in that it enables us to "make sense of our own past experiences" and "explore possible future realities" crucial in decision-making. In other words, we imagine several future possibilities, weigh them against memories of our past experiences, and pick one that seems best. We humans confabulate; we fill gaps of memory with plausible inventions in order to preserve continuity. Evolution seems to have hard-wired our brains for storytelling because it has helped us survive. We are not stronger or faster than other species; we don't have special sensory skills. But storytelling enables us to form memories and project future outcomes. And it forms the basis for our consciousness and makes us self-aware. And all this occurred, I am guessing, either shortly before *Homo sapiens* gained language or at approximately the same time. Perhaps our ability to tell ourselves stories was the impetus to share those stories with others.

Language acquisition. According to an article in a 2006 Special Edition of *Scientific American,* "How We Came to be Human," Ian Tattersall speculates that humans "had a vocal tract that could produce the sounds of articulate speech over half a million years before we have evidence our forebears used language," a phenomenon he puts at about 70,000 YA (years ago) when the earliest evidences of symbolic thought began to surface. According to Tattersall, this enabled language to spread quickly. Not all scientists agree with him on this count. According to the Smithsonian website, human language may date back to about 350,000 YA when humans began making stone tools and coloring objects.

Spoken language became possible when the voice box dropped lower in the throat and the area above the vocal chords lengthened, which enabled us to make a wide variety of sounds. However, when that happened, it became impossible to swallow and breathe at the same time, often causing the individual to choke. Interestingly, human babies do not have a lowered voice box and can breathe while nursing like other mammal babies. In any case, sounds (perhaps imitating bird or animal sounds) and gesture probably preceded language.

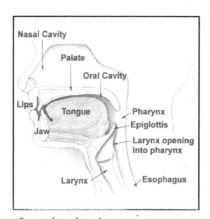

Anatomy of mouth and neck.
http://commons.wikimedia.org/wiki/File:Illu01_head_neck.jpg
By Arcadian [Public domain], via Wikimedia Commons

Research in neuroscience. The brain's wiring for stories is now becoming evident, thanks to new evidence in neuroscientific research, most recently from fMRI studies (functional Magnetic Resonance Imaging) that measure brain activity by detecting changes in blood flow and indicating neural activity as specific tasks are performed. The ability to link neural activity to the tasks of reading, listening, or viewing information and stories has produced some startling revelations. When we are presented with "information" (facts, figures, power points), only two areas of the brain, the Wernicke's area and the Broca's area, light up. Both areas have to do with language processing and comprehension. According to Jenny Nabben in "The Science behind Storytelling," it is difficult for the brain to decode, process, and remember abstract or conceptual information. So, we have no inclination to remember or act on such information because it takes so much energy to decode it and because we have no emotional involvement with the information presented.

However, in major studies at Princeton University in 2012, Uri Hassan and his team of psychologists studied a phenomenon they call "coupling"; they found that the brain of the storyteller and the brain of the listener become inextricably linked during the storytelling experience. They discovered in fMRI studies conducted during storytelling that, whether the story is fact or fiction, multiple brain regions become activated: the motor cortex (physical movements), olfactory cortex (smell), visual cortex (color, shape) and auditory cortex (sound). These areas work together to build rich images that engage the emotions, and emotional associations are known to trump all other forms of mental processing. The amygdala, the integrative center for the emotions, emotional behavior, and motivation, is activated to evoke both emotional responses and past emotional memories that enable us to put ourselves in the shoes of various characters. Hassan's research has shown that the listener experiences almost *identical brain responses* as the *person telling the story* AND *the person actually having such an experience.*

This is the way the storytelling experience seems to work on the part of the listener (I will use "listener" to mean also viewer, reader). Because sensory-specific words are used to tell a story, multi-sensory cortices are activated in the brain and the brain "imagines" the experience. As tension builds and the listener's attention is sustained, emotions are neurologically activated, and the listener develops an emotional association with the character; as the story's structure is recognized (beginning, middle, end), the listener becomes emotionally absorbed in the character's story and begins to mimic the character's behavior or perspective. The listener can even change his/her own behavior or perspective as a result. As an added benefit, the experience is more often than not committed to memory so that it can be recalled for future use.

Neurochemicals and Storytelling. The activation of certain areas of the brain when listening to a story depends in part on various neurochemicals. Two key components are *cortisol* and *oxytocin*. *Cortisol* is a chemical released when people feel distress or experience tension when a story is being told. *Cortisol* captures the listener's attention long enough for the subsequent synthesis of *oxytocin*. In 2012 Paul J. Zak, an American economist, identified the role oxytocin plays in mediating trust between unacquainted humans. His extensive research showed that this neurochemical produces an "it's safe to approach others" attitude toward unknown adults, motivates cooperation, enhances empathy, and makes us more sensitive to social clues.

Listening to character-driven stories produces *oxytocin synthesis*, a process that continues as tension in the story mounts. If this tension is sustained long enough, the listener begins to *share the emotions* of the character(s) and experiences empathy. The impact of the entire storytelling experience is exponential. In his article "How Stories Change the Brain", Zak argues that stories can indeed change the brain. Once the listener's attention is captured and oxytocin synthesis sustained, the listener begins to *mimic the feelings and behaviors* of the characters, an emotional involvement Zak calls "transportation." He sees it as "an amazing neural feat" that comes from oxytocin synthesis deep within ancient parts of the brain that causes us to "simulate" emotions we intuit for the characters, emotions that we feel as well, which in turn "change the brain."

The storytelling experience is also accompanied by the production and release of *dopamine*, a neurochemical responsible for reward, pleasure, goal setting, motivation, and, not surprisingly, addiction. Additionally, the element of surprise in a story can become like candy to the listener; it triggers the release of *adrenaline* in the brain, which heightens memory formation. The best stories motivate us to make behavioral changes, engage with others, and remember the lessons for future decision-making.

Becoming Human. We must assume that human beings have been telling stories to themselves and each other at least since we acquired language if not before. According to Edward O. Wilson, one of the world's leading biologists and author of *The Meaning of Human Existence* (2014), the "altruistic division of labor at a protected nest site" (meaning shared responsibility in a species community) has occurred in only twenty species since the beginning of life some four billion years ago: fourteen of these species are insects; three are coral-dwelling marine shrimp; and three are mammals. Of the mammals, two are African mole rats. The third is *Homo sapiens*. *Homo sapiens* had the advantages of upright walking, a large brain cavity (able to evolve the storytelling function), digital dexterity, and an audio-visual method of communication. "Of the many thousands of large terrestrial animal species that have flourished on Earth for the past four hundred million years," Wilson explains, only *Homo sapiens* made the ascent. Only humans developed social units, organized political systems to manage them, and evoked great religions to guide their behavior.

The Smithsonian Institution depicts the "Homo" group on "The Human Family Tree" as consisting of seven separate species. Of these, three other species overlap with us, *Homo sapiens: Homo floresiensis* (the "hobbit" of Indonesia), the *Denisovans,* and *Homo neanderthalensis.* The big question is why did *Homo sapiens* win out while the others became extinct? Why did *Homo sapiens* become the one who ascended to dominate our planet? Though other factors were surely involved, the evidence is beginning to suggest that either we were *the best storytelling species* or we were the *only storytelling species.* Storytelling may be the defining factor in the ascent of *Homo sapiens* and our domination of the planet Earth.

My View: *Homo sapiens'* storytelling abilities catapulted him ahead of his competitors. All four species walked upright; all four had digital dexterity, an audio-visual method of gaining information about their environment; all four had large brains. In fact, *Homo sapiens'* brain was *smaller* than that of *Homo neanderthalensis.* Plus *Homo neanderthalensis* was stockier, sturdier in build. And he did make tools and bury his dead. So what gave *Homo sapiens* the advantage? What made *Homo sapiens* surperior?

Perhaps his brain was more nimble, more suitable for storytelling. E. O. Wilson's vast scientific experiences indicate that "confabulation" is a human necessity: 1) it facilitates our ability to process the myriad bits of sensory information brought into our brains (research by Gazzaniga and other neuroscientists back this up), and 2) it allows us to "summon the stories of past events for context and meaning," and use these stories to create "multiple competing scenarios" on which choices are made. In *The Meaning of Human Existence* Wilson maintains, "Conscious mental life is built entirely from confabulation" (167).

Confabulation: storytelling.

Most experts put the outside limits of what we call "human behavior" at about 100,000 years ago. Most agree on sometime between 60,000 and 40,000 YA for the emergence of symbolic thought in "story" form—the carvings of humans and animals, for example. The oldest of the human carvings is the Venus of Willendorf in 28,000-25,000 BCE (Before Current Era—used to be BC, Before Christ) found in Germany. This is a very small object only 4 inches tall.

Willendorf Venus.
https://commons.wikimedia.org/wiki/File:Willendorf-Venus-1468.jpg
By Don Hitchcock (Own work) [CC BY-SA 3.0 (http://creativecommons.org/licenses/by-sa/3.0)], via Wikimedia Commons

The making of human ornamentation in the form of beads dates from 70,000 BCE and were found in Blombos Cave in South Africa.

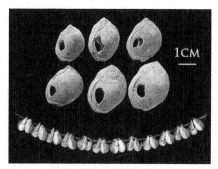

Blombos Cave shell ornaments and beads.
https://commons.wikimedia.org/wiki/File:Blombos_Cave_marine_shell_beads.jpg
By Marian Vanhaeren & Christopher S. Henshilwood (Own work)
[CC BY-SA 3.0 (http://creativecommons.org/licenses/by-sa/3.0)],
via Wikimedia Commons

Probably the most astounding finds are the cave paintings in France and Spain. Here's an image from the caves at Lascaux, France, some of the most spectacular paintings yet discovered (17,000 BCE):

Lascaux cave painting.
http://commons.wikimedia.org/wiki/File:Lascaux_painting.jpg
By Prof saxx (Own work) [GFDL (http://www.gnu.org/copyleft/fdl.html)
or CC-BY-SA-3.0 (http://creativecommons.org/licenses/by-sa/3.0/)],
via Wikimedia Commons

In addition to the visual arts, some of the oldest musical instruments found are even older than the paintings on the Lascaux cave walls. This flute, one of the earliest instrument found to date, is from the Geissenklösterle Cave in Germany; it is 35,000 to 43,000 years old.

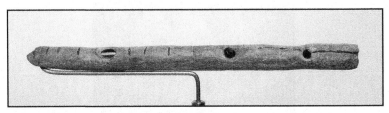

Bone flute dated in the Upper Paleolithic from Geissenklösterle.
https://commons.wikimedia.org/wiki/File:Flauta_paleol%C3%ADtica.jpg
José-Manuel Benito Álvarez [CC BY-SA 2.5 (http://creativecommons.org/licenses/by-sa/2.5)], via Wikimedia Commons

Though experts may disagree on what "stories" these artifacts tell, all agree that "storytelling" was the aim. Communicating experience: physical, emotional, spiritual. Most agree as well that the emergence of at least some of the "humanities" occurred almost simultaneously about 50,000 YA: *Homo sapiens* began painting on cave walls, making music, and ritually burying the dead (putting ornaments, flowers, weapons with the dead in the grave).

Homo sapiens came out of Africa about 60,000 YA and literally exploded on the scene. But he was not alone. At least two other species of hominid cousins walked the Eurasian landmass—Neanderthals and Denisovans. Our ancestors encountered the Neanderthals and inbred with them and so a small amount of Neanderthal DNA was introduced into the modern human gene pool. Europeans and Asians have between 1 to 4 percent Neanderthal DNA. Indigenous sub-Saharan Africans have no Neanderthal DNA because their ancestors did not migrate through Eurasia. The Denisovans went to Sibera and Asia, but were fewer in numbers and traces of Denisovan DNA have been found in modern humans. The Neanderthals died out about 30,000 YA, only a few thousand years after modern humans arrived in Europe. Perhaps *Homo sapiens'* storytelling abilities allowed him to outsmart his competitors.

Prehistoric Stories. Looking backward forty or fifty thousand years, we may wonder what kinds of stories our prehistoric ancestors told. Some of these are recorded in paintings on cave walls, in ornaments, in the carvings of humans and animals, in the musical instruments left behind. Some told of great hunts and near death experiences; some recounted the feats of men of great daring, the heroes of the tribe. And some, no doubt attained the status of myth.

The Greek word *mythos* means "story" or "word." The term "myth" has come to refer to a certain genre (category) of stories. A myth is a symbolic tale of the distant past. Myths 1) explain the Origin of the Universe and beings in that universe, 2) are connected to the Sacred and to Ritual, 3) reflect Social Order or Values within a culture, 4) provide a way to understand Nature, 5) involve Heroic Characters like proto-humans, super humans, gods) who mediate and establish patterns of life, and 6) reflect actors and actions outside routine experience. This is all according to Joseph Campbell, an expert on comparative religions of the world. In the PBS series *The Power of Myth*, he defines mythology as a "system of images that incorporates a concept of the universe that acts as a divinely energized or energizing presence in the world we live in." A myth, he says, is not simply a story, but is "inspired" by nature and exists below the level of consciousness of which we are aware. It's "a message from the unconscious to the consciousness," the first function of which is to inspire awe in the individual and a sense of wonder at one's participation in the universe. Myth also serves as a guide for the individual's social, moral, and spiritual conduct in society. Campbell maintains that myth reflects an awakening invoked simultaneously as human beings gained a sense of consciousness (self-awareness), and, as we have seen, consciousness is coincidental with the storytelling impulse. Myth is a story on steroids, a hyper-energized story. There is every reason to believe that our prehistoric ancestors were mythological storytellers, at least in part, as illustrated in their oral literature, in their paintings on cave walls, in the miniature statues of animals and themselves, in the music they made with primitive instruments, and in the ritual burials of their dead.

Part II: The Civilizing Force

Most evolutionary biologists agree that storytelling became hardwired into our human brains because it served a practical function necessary for survival. Storytelling enabled early humans to piece together useful information, to pass on details about tool-making, hunting and gathering, and to synthesize the neurochemical oxytocin that fosters social cooperation. Storytelling made possible the formation of social units (tribes, towns, nations) cultivated by a cooperative spirit and enabled humans to develop social units, organize political systems to manage them, and establish religions to guide them. No society persists without passing on its social values in story form. No political group rises to power without a story that resonates with its constituents. Try to imagine a religion that would not at its core have a great story, a story that allows participants to step outside themselves, to connect with a larger world and universal truths, to share in a narrative that transcends generations.

Revolutions led to "Civilized" life. The *Neolithic Revolution* marked a fundamental shift from hunting and gathering to agriculture, permanent settlements, and the rise of civilizations. The earliest known villages ca. 9000 BCE were groups of sedentary hunter-gathers who settled around Jericho and Abu Hereryra. Neolithic cultures domesticated the first plants (ca. 8300-7500 BCE) and then animals (ca. 7500-6000 BCE). According to Joseph Campbell, myths involving regeneration and transformation emerged when people turned from being primarily hunters (when the animal is killed, it is dead) to domesticating plants (when one harvests a plant, it continues to grow and produce). These people used flint tools, engaged in

17

trade, and developed *"ancestor cults"* that emphasized the possession of land. About 6000 BCE, these foundations gave rise to an *Urban Revolution* across the Middle East as farming and herding produced surplus food, engendered craft specialists, priests, and political leaders, and triggered the emergence of economic inequalities and social classes. The earliest civilizations appeared in an area called the Fertile Crescent along the Tigris and Euphrates Rivers to the east (Phoenicia, Assyria, and Mesopotamia—now Iraq) and along the Nile in Egypt.

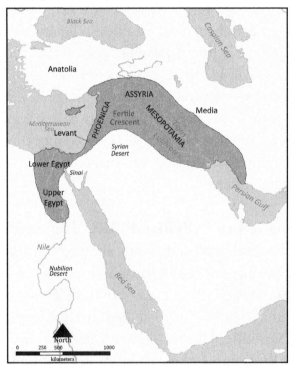

The Fertile Crescent.
https://commons.wikimedia.org/wiki/File:Map_of_fertile_crescent.svg
By Nafsadh (Map of fertile cresent.png) [GFDL (http://www.gnu.org/copyleft/fdl.html)
or CC BY-SA 4.0-3.0-2.5-2.0-1.0 (http://creativecommons.org/licenses/by-sa/
4.0-3.0-2.5-2.0-1.0)], via Wikimedia Commons

All civilizations share certain characteristics: 1) large population centers, 2) monumental architecture and unique art styles, 3) a state religion or ideology, 4) a system for administering territories (a political system), 5) a complex division of labor, 6) the division of people into social classes (including a ruling class exempt from manual labor), and 7) *a system for recording information.*

A System for Recording Information. The earliest true writing system is found in the cuneiform tablets of the Sumerians ca. 3200 BCE in Mesopotamia (Iraq). First used to record transactions, writing systems became a new dimension in storytelling, one that could pass on records of the past to future generations without relying on the memory of the Keeper of tribal tales. For the first time, storytellers could connect with listeners as yet unborn. The earliest writings in almost all cultures recorded accounting of some sort: money owed or delivered, grain sold or stored. Only later did people begin to record historical events and finally the stories and myths of their people. The *Epic of Gilgamesh*, the first great work of literature, was set down in the cuneiform language ca. 1850 BCE in Mesopotamia. It is a story that shares similarities with stories that record the early Jewish religious experience now parts of the *Torah* (the Pentateuch), the *Bible*, and the *Quran*.

Tablet V of the *Epic of Gilgamesh*, from the old Babylonian period, 2003-1595 BCE.
https://commons.wikimedia.org/wiki/File:Tablet_V_of_the_Epic_of_Gligamesh.JPG
By Osama Shukir Muhammed Amin FRCP(Glasg) (Own work) [CC BY-SA 4.0 (http://
creativecommons.org/licenses/by-sa/4.0)], via Wikimedia Commons

Stories, Myths, and Religion. It is no wonder, then, that shortly after the rise of civilizations in the Middle East, the world's great religions began to emerge around some of the most powerful stories every told. Recall that, according to Joseph Campbell, myth is a specific genre of story that serves to awaken "a sense of awe and mystery in the universe." He expands on this idea, suggesting that myth furnishes a recognition of elementary ideas inherent in the cosmos, validates a moral system within the community concerning the supernatural or the sacred, and acts as a guide of individuals through the "passages of human life" (from birth and dependency in childhood, to the responsibility of adulthood, to the "ultimate passage" through old age and death). Myth does this via "universal themes and motifs." However, *religion* is a broader term that includes myth along with ritual, a moral code, some type of mystical experience, and a theology (which systemizes and provides a means for the study of religious truth and divinity).

Abraham's story is crucial to three great religions, Judaism, Christianity, and Islam. It recounts Abraham's journey from Ur to Canaan, a journey he began about 1850 BCE, about the same time the *Epic of Gilgamesh* was written down. Abraham's story, though preserved orally, was not written down until about the tenth century BCE after the Israelites' liberation from Egypt under Moses' leadership and their resettlement in Canaan. These accounts did not exist in their current form until after the Babylonian Captivity of the Israelites that ended in 538 BCE. Though accounts vary in the *Torah*, the *Bible*, and the *Quran*, Abraham's story is the foundation of all three religions and for millennium has captured the imaginations of Christians (32% of the world's population), Muslims (23%), and Jews (2%).

Up to this time, human beings from prehistoric man to his more modern descendants two millennia BCE had been preoccupied with cyclical myths. These were no doubt influenced by the observance of the swirling night sky and nature's seasonal cycles. However, Abraham's story tells a brand new tale, one never before told. Instead of the organization that represented the ancient worldview in which the story's pattern follows a circle, a cycle, and comes back to where it began, Abraham's story is linear: it has a beginning, a middle, and an end. It possesses the very structure that we internally expect of a story.

In Abraham's story God speaks to Abram (his name at the time) and commands him to "go forth"—away from the predictable cycle of many gods in his polytheistic Semite urban city of Ur—and begin a journey into an unknown wilderness. God does not tell Abram where he is going. As a single deity,

God intervenes in human history and changes the journey of human kind. It was a new story, a story never before told.

Below is a summary of Thomas Cahill's account of Abraham's Story as told in Cahill's book, *The Gifts of the Jews: How a Tribe of Desert Nomads Changed the Way Everyone Thinks and Feels* (1998).

Abram was a Semite. When God speaks to him and commands him to "go forth," Abram goes. He packs up his family and leaves his home in Ur for an undisclosed destination. God tells Abram along the way that his current childless marriage will produce "a great nation," that all humanity will eventually find its blessings through him. Abram and his family settle for a time in Harran where they gain great wealth, but eventually they leave Harran. These once sophisticated urbanites from Ur continue as wanderers in a wilderness. Eventually they settle in Canaan, another land of Semitic tribes, but tribes much less civilized than those in Ur. When famine strikes, Abram heads for Egypt, an even more alien territory, where Sara (Abram's childless wife) poses as his sister and is taken into the Pharaoh's harem. Abram's God sends a plague on Egypt in retaliation; Abram and his family are blamed and sent out of Egypt. Eventually Abram fathers two children: Ishmael, the son of Sara's servant Hagar, and then miraculously Isaac, the son of Sara who is way past childbearing age by this time.

After the destruction of Sodom and Gomorrah, Abram faces a final test: He must take his son Isaac to the Mountain and sacrifice Isaac to God. This gets Abram's full attention. As Abram prepares to make the sacrifice, God stops him and furnishes him instead with a goat. At this point, Abram experiences an awakening. He realizes that, while he began as a Sumerian polytheist (a believer in many gods), he became a monotheist (a believer in one god) as he gained a new personal relationship with God, a single divine entity. Abram's consciousness has been altered; he has moved beyond the ritual and earthly images of the Sumerian gods and toward a personal relationship with a single God. His faith has opened him to possibility. As a reward, Abram's name is changed to Abraham in honor of the new person he has become.

Abraham's story, the story of a single man's journey, was unlike any previous stories of heroes' journeys. Abraham's journey was singular, deliberate, and obedient. More importantly, God was the journey's Initiator; God begins the dialogue with man. And, Cahill maintains, "Abraham's story is real history." After Abraham's journey, Cahill says, "time is no longer cyclical but one-way and irreversible." After Abraham's story, personal history is possible and the individual has value. That's the power of Abraham's story. By the point in history in which we find ourselves today, Abraham's story has changed the lives of more than half the people on the Earth.

Egypt. Egypt is one of the oldest civilizations on earth. It's probably best known for its pyramids that tell a story of their own. The Giza pyramids, the most famous, are among the oldest. The largest of the three pyramids at Giza, known as the Great Pyramid, was built for Khufu between 2474-2566 BCE. Its sides are oriented to the four cardinal points on the compass (N, S, E, W). Approximately 2,300,000 limestone blocks, each weighing an average of 2.5 tons, were used. The Great pyramid was encased in smooth limestone, but this was plundered in our era to build Cairo. The second pyramid (that appears taller but isn't) was build for Khufu's son, Khafre. The Great Sphinx was also built for Khafre and is part of Khafre's pyramid complex in honor of the sun god. Khafre's son built the third pyramid at the Giza site.

Pyramids of Giza and sphinx.
https://commons.wikimedia.org/wiki/File:Egypt.Giza.Sphinx.02.jpg
By Most likely Hamish2k, the first uploader (Most likely Hamish2k, the first uploader) [GFDL (http://www.gnu.org/copyleft/fdl.html) or CC-BY-SA-3.0 (http://creativecommons.org/licenses/by-sa/3.0/)], via Wikimedia Commons

Abraham "sojourned" in Egypt around 1850 BCE, about 700 years after the Giza pyramids were built, and 600 years after Abraham returned to Canaan, the land that God promised him, Ramses II became pharaoh of Egypt. Ramses II serves in part as a continuation of Abraham's story. Ramses II was likely pharaoh of Egypt when the "Children of Israel" were enslaved and when Moses led the Israelites out of bondage, through the Red Sea, and into the Sinai desert where Moses received the Ten Commandments from God on Mt. Sinai.

Ramses II reigned from 1279-1213 BCE and was one of the most powerful rulers in all of Egypt. He was a builder, determined to convince himself and everyone else that he was a deity. He was the third pharaoh of the 19th dynasty of the New Kingdom and ruled an amazing 67 years. His architectural accomplishments were astounding. He erected more monuments than any other ancient Egyptian pharaoh. He built an immense Ramesseum, a memorial temple complex located near Luxor.

Ruins of Ramesseum.

Even more impressive is the enormous Ramses II statue unearthed at Memphis (below); it was commissioned by Ramses II and demonstrates the huge impact Ramses the Great had on the artwork of his day. Here is the remains of the statue with a person standing near that indicates the statue's enormous size:

Ramses II statue at Memphis.
https://commons.wikimedia.org/wiki/File%3AEgypt-Memphis-Giant-Ramses-II.jpg
By Barrylb at en.wikipedia [Public domain], from Wikimedia Commons

Abu Simbel, one of Ramses II's most crowning achievements, was built during a twenty-year period between 1264 and 1224 BCE. It is, in fact, two temples. The larger is Ramses II's temple; the smaller adjacent temple was built for his favorite wife, Queen Nefertari. Originally cut into a solid rock cliff in southern Egypt along the Nile River, most experts agree that the structures were created, at least in part, to celebrate Rameses' victory over the Hittites at the Battle of Kadesh in 1274 BCE; extensive art work throughout the interior of the Great Temple depict this battle. Its location, on the border with the conquered lands of Nubia, suggests to some that it would have been built after the Nubian Campaigns. The Great

Temple is dedicated to the gods Ra-Horakty, Ptah, and the deified Rameses II, while the smaller one designed for Queen Nefertari, Ramses' favorite wife, is dedicated to the goddess Hathor.

Entrance to Abu Simbel.
https://commons.wikimedia.org/wiki/File:Abu_Simbel_Temple_May_30_2007.jpg
By Than217 at English Wikipedia (Transferred from en.wikipedia to Commons.)
[Public domain], via Wikimedia Commons

The image above is the entrance to the Great Temple; all four figures are gigantic carvings of Ramses II on this throne. The enormous size of the temple's entrance is evident. Beneath these giant figures of Ramses II are larger-than-life-sized statues representing Rames II's conquered enemies, the Nubians, Libyans, and Hittites. Inside the temple are detailed depictions of the events surrounding the Battle of Kadesh and the defeat of the Hitties. In one famous depiction of the battle, Ramses II takes on the whole Hittite army single-handedly, supported only by Amun [the god] who hands him the victory. Also, deep inside the temple sit three gods along with Ramses II. In the inner sanctuary on February 22 and October 22 of each year, the sunlight shines on that particular spot, illuminating the deified Ramses II, Amon-Re, and Ptah, but keeping Re-Harakhti, god of the dead, in shadow. The exterior tells a story to those who view it from afar; the interior holds a wealth of other tales. The temple's interior also contains eight giant pillars depicting Osiris, god of the dead as well as god of resurrection and fertility.

Temple of Ramses II with the eight pillars of Osiris.
https://commons.wikimedia.org/wiki/File%3ATemple_of_Rameses_II %2C_eight_Osiris_pillars.jpg
By Dennis Jarvis from Halifax, Canada (Egypt-10C-037 Uploaded by PDTillman) [CC BY-SA 2.0 (http://creativecommons.org/licenses/by-sa/2.0)], via Wikimedia Commons

In the case of Abu Simbel, there are other stories as well. By the 6th century BCE, the Great Temple was already covered in sand up to the knees of the statues and both temples were forgotten. Over two thousand years later, in 1813, Swiss scholar, Johann Burckhardt was traveling down the Nile when he saw the front of the great temple though the rest of it was buried in sand. He told his friend, and Italian explorer Giovanni Belzoni. It was not until 1817 that the English explorer and Egyptologist William John Bankes was able to excavate and enter the base of the monument.

Lantern Slide Collection colored slide of Abu Simbel covered in sand.
https://commons.wikimedia.org/wiki/File%3AS10_08_Abu_Simbel
%2C_image_9491.jpg
William Henry Goodyear [Public domain], via Wikimedia Commons

However, that is not the end of the story. In the 1960s, the Egyptian government decided to build the Aswan High Dam on the Nile River. The project threatened to submerge the temples of Abu Simbel. This led to one of the most famous and difficult engineering feats ever attempted: the dismantling, moving, and reassembling of the two temples while retaining the exact, original orientation that they had held to each other and to the sun.

Dismantling Abu Simbel statues.
https://commons.wikimedia.org/wiki/File%3AAbusimbel.jpg
By "Per-Olow" - Per-Olow Anderson (1921-1989) (sv:Forskning & Framsteg 1967 issue 3, page 16) [Public domain], via Wikimedia Commons

The temples were carved into many pieces and moved up the sandstone cliff 60 meters from their original location.

Stories that Changed the World do not exist in isolation. They are collective and encapsulate many related stories that take us backward and forward in time.

Greece. The Egyptian Civilization was not the only ancient civilization to tell its story to the world. By 900 BCE, the Greek Civilization was rising to power. Even so, the Greeks had been around for a long time. Between 3000-1100 BCE, the Minoans and the Mycenaeans were organizing themselves into the beginning of what we now call "western civilization." The Minoans (ca. 2000-1500 BCE) became the foundation for the first Greek civilization and established themselves on the island of Crete. The Greeks who settled on Crete were influenced by the earlier Near Eastern civilizations of Mesopotamia (Abraham's world), Egypt (Ramses II's world), and the peoples of the Cycladic islands. The Minoans were very sophisticated (had water pipes and toilets with pipes leading to outside drains), but their civilization came to a sudden and mysterious end, probably due to a massive volcanic eruption on a nearby island and the enormous tidal wave that followed. The Minoans worshiped the bull and practiced "bull jumping." Their name comes from the legendary King Minos who built the Labyrinth (maze) to house the legendary beast, the Minotaur (half man, half bull). The image below was found in the Knossos palace on Crete and dates to 1600-1400 BCE. The Lost Continent Atlantis is associated with the Minoans and their civilization on Crete. The Mycenaens ascended to power (ca. 1500-1100 BCE) but established their civilization on the European continent where Greece exists today. These cultures laid the foundation for the classical Greeks who followed them with one of the world's great civilizations.

Minoan Bull from Crete, 1600-1400 BCE.
https://commons.wikimedia.org/wiki/File%3AAMI_-_Stierrhyton.jpg
By Wolfgang Sauber (Own work) [GFDL (http://www.gnu.org/copyleft/fdl.html) or CC BY-SA 3.0 (http://creativecommons.org/licenses/by-sa/3.0)], via Wikimedia Commons

Highlights of the Greek Civilization include many stories: the Greek myths, numerous famous monuments like the Parthenon, the epics of the *Illiad* and the *Odyssey* (written down by Homer ca. 750-700 BCE). Taken together the two works recount the story of the Trojan War (ca. 1184 BCE), its heroes, and the gods who helped each side during the Greek attempt to rescue the famous Helen from her Trojan captors. Pericles (460-430 BCE) ushered in the Golden Age of Greece, ruled Athens, and strengthened democracy during his reign. He was responsible for the building of the Parthenon (447-432 BCE), a temple dedicated to the goddess Athena.

The Parthenon.
https://commons.wikimedia.org/wiki/File:The_Parthenon_in_Athens.jpg
By Steve Swayne [CC BY 2.0 (http://creativecommons.org/licenses/by/2.0)],
via Wikimedia Commons

The Parthenon was built on the Acropolis, a huge outcropping in the center of Athens that rises 490 feet in the air and has a surface area of 7 acres; it was fortified and inhabited at least by 1900-1100 BCE.

Acropolis Hill.
https://commons.wikimedia.org/wiki/
File:Attica_06-13_Athens_50_View_from_Philopappos_-_Acropolis_Hill.jpg
A.Savin [CC BY-SA 3.0 (http://creativecommons.org/licenses/by-sa/3.0) or FAL],
via Wikimedia Commons

Below the Parthenon and the wall fortifying it are two theaters; theaters were an integral part of Greek religious worship. The one below is the Theater of Dionysus. Dionysus was the god of wine and also the source of the belief in rebirth after death.

The Dionysian Festival was held each year and a drama competition was a part of that festival augmented by religious rituals held over from prehistoric times.

Theater of Dionysus at the Acropolis of Athens.
https://commons.wikimedia.org/wiki/File%3ADionisov_teatar_u_Akropolju.jpg
Wikipedia user Славен Косановић [GFDL (http://www.gnu.org/copyleft/fdl.html)
or CC-BY-SA-3.0 (http://creativecommons.org/licenses/by-sa/3.0/)],
from Wikimedia Commons

Among the celebrities of Greece are three philosophers. **Socrates** lived ca. 469-399 BCE during the period of the city's greatest cultural expansion. He was well-known in Athens for his non-traditional teaching methods known now as the "Socratic Method" of asking questions and leading the student to a logical answer. When a power struggle ensued, Socrates was accused of corrupting the minds of youth, and when he refused to recant his beliefs, he accepted death over exile, drinking the poisoned hemlock that ended his life.

Plato (ca. 427-347 BCE) was Socrates' student. He was born into a noble Athenian family but grew up during a civil war at the end of the Athenian Golden Age. After Socrates' death, Plato gave up political aspirations and became a philosopher. In 386 BCE, he founded his Academy, among the first organized institutions of higher education in the Western world. There he taught and wrote, completing his most famous work, *The Republic*, in 347 BCE. Particularly influential was his theory of Forms. Plato suggested that the material world (i.e., a chair) is based on a metaphysical reality of ideas that exists in an eternal world of Forms (i.e., somewhere there is an ideal chair, or an idea of *chairness*, that enables us in this world to identify a chair). He had a similar idea of an absolute Form of the Good that came very close to the Christian notion of a monotheistic God even though he lived centuries before the birth of Christ. Plato's "Allegory of the Cave" is a very famous "story" from *The Republic*; it is an allegory highlighting the benefits of education.

Plato's most famous pupil was **Aristotle** (ca. 384-322 BCE). Even though he was not an Athenian citizen, he spent most of his life in Athens and was considered to be Plato's successor. He bypassed that opportunity and, after some travels that included zoological observations and marine experiments in biology and his three years as **Alexander the Great's** tutor, he returned to Athens and founded his own school, the Lyceum, in 355 BCE after Alexander assumed the throne. Alexander supported the Lyceum and gave Aristotle the freedom to pursue scientific and philosophic interests. Aristotle developed a course of study that resembles the modern Western university system. Aristotle repudiated Plato's metaphysical understanding of the world and developed processes of scientific observation and experimentation, establishing systems and categories of scholarly research that survive to the present day. He also espoused the idea of the "Golden Mean" which finds the middle road between two extremes the most desirable. For example, *courage* is the "mean" (middle) between the extremes of *recklessness* (excess of courage) and *cowardice* (deficiency of courage). After Alexander the Great's death in 323 BCE in Egypt, Aristotle fled from Athens and died shortly after.

Part III: God and Man

A lot happens between Plato's "Allegory of the Cave" (347 BCE) and the beginning of the Middle Ages in Europe. **The Roman Empire** happened, and during that time, Jesus was born and crucified generating a story (a continuation of Abraham's) that still resonates with 32% of the world's population who practice Christianity today, 2000 years later. The founding of Rome goes back to the early days of civilization, but the Roman Empire officially began in 49 BCE when Julius Caesar, a Roman politician and general, conquered the vast territory of the Gauls to the north of his province in France. His military campaigns took him to Egypt where he met Cleopatra. He was famously murdered in the Senate in 44 BCE.

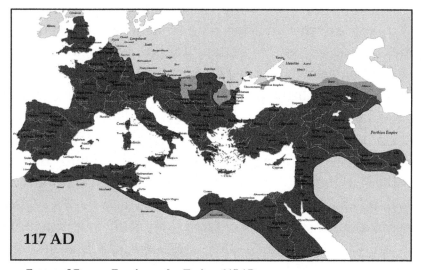

Extent of Roman Empire under Trajan, 117 AD.
https://commons.wikimedia.org/wiki/File:Roman_Empire_Trajan_117AD.png
By Tataryn77 (Own work) [CC BY-SA 3.0 (http://creativecommons.org/licenses/by-sa/3.0)], via Wikimedia Commons

However, the Roman Empire flourished and at its height in 117 AD with the Emperor Trajan in charge, it extended from

Babylonia in the Middle East through all of Mesopotamia, Turkey, Armenia, almost all of Europe, most of Great Britain, and all of Northern Africa including Egypt and the Holy Land. In fact, Rome was ruled in two distinct parts: The Western Roman Empire and the Eastern Roman Empire. The Eastern Roman Empire was known as the **Byzantine Empire** and outlasted the Western Roman Empire by almost a thousand years. In 410 AD, the city of Rome was sacked by the Visigoths (Germanic Tribes). These tribes from Northern Europe had been looting, raping, and pillaging parts of the Western Roman Empire for a couple of centuries; by 476, they overthrew the last of the Roman emperors in the West. Even as the Roman Empire of the West fell, the Byzantine Empire in the East flourished. This is primarily because its emperor, Constantine, became a Christian in 313 AD and ended all persecution of Christians. The Western Roman Empire was Christian too, but these people spoke Latin and were guided by the Church in Rome. People in the Byzantine Empire spoke Greek and worshiped under what is now known as the Eastern Orthodox branch of the Christian Church. In 324 AD, Constantine became emperor of the Eastern Empire, naming his city Constantinople (the "city of Constanine"—now Istanbul, Turkey). Over the next centuries, the Byzantine Empire flourished while the Western Empire declined. This time in Europe is often called the "Dark Ages" because the Germanic Tribes had taken over and terrorized most of the population. In fact, the Christian church almost disappeared from Europe during this time.

Stories of God: The Middle Ages in Europe

Enter **Saint Augustine**, the Benedictine monk who became the first Archbishop of Canterbury in 597 AD. He is not to be confused with St. Augustine of Hippo, the more famous of the two and the author of *City of God*. Augustine of Canterbury was sent by Pope Gregory the Great to convert King Æthelberht and his Kingdom of Kent from Anglo-Saxon paganism. This Augustine did, probably with the help of the King's Christian wife, Bertha, and Æthelberht allowed Augustine and his missionaries to settle and preach in Canterbury. They used the church of St. Martin's for services and soon after Augustine's arrival, he founded the monastery that became St. Augustine's Abby. Both structures are preserved as part of the **Canterbury Cathedral** UNESCO site.

St. Martin's at Canterbury.
https://commons.wikimedia.org/wiki/File:Canterbury_St_Martin_close.jpg
By Oosoom (Self-photographed) [GFDL (http://www.gnu.org/copyleft/fdl.html)
or CC BY-SA 3.0 (http://creativecommons.org/licenses/by-sa/3.0)],
via Wikimedia Commons

Ruins of the rotunda and nave of the Church of St. Peter and Paul at St. Augustine's Abbey.
https://commons.wikimedia.org/wiki/File:Staugustinescanterburyrotundaandnave.jpg
By Ealdgyth (Own work) [CC BY-SA 3.0 (http://creativecommons.org/licenses/by-sa/3.0)], via Wikimedia Commons

The first Cathedral in Canterbury was in fact built by St. Augustine around 597 AD. That Cathedral and later Anglo-Saxon replacements have all been lost to view; the remains are hidden under the present building. The Cathedral we see today dates from 1070 at the earliest, just after the Norman Conquest (1066) when the French conquered the last Anglo-Saxon King at the Battle of Hastings and brought a French influence to England.

Canterbury Cathedral.
https://commons.wikimedia.org/wiki/File:Canterbury_Cathedral_001.jpg
By Nilfanion (Own work) [CC BY-SA 4.0 (http://creativecommons.org/licenses/by-sa/4.0)], via Wikimedia Commons

Most of the great cathedrals of Europe were built in the Middle Ages between 1050 and 1350. The story they told was of God, as almost all stories told in the Middle Ages were. It was a God-centered Universe, and man was considered insignificant in the cosmic scheme. Churches took several generations to build (80-100 years) and were constructed to get this message across. Going into one of these cathedrals does indeed put one in one's place. Moreover, the Church was the center of community life, as is evident in the photograph above. The cathedrals were built in the center and the town grew up around it, solidifying its central position. Each church was (and still is, for the most part—check your church out) built on an East-West axis with the altar and apse at the East and the main entrance at the West. Notice the following diagram. What shape does the floor plan have? Do you recognize it? Why do you think it has this shape? Lesson number one about the stories by cathedrals: every detail is a religious symbol that helps tell God's story.

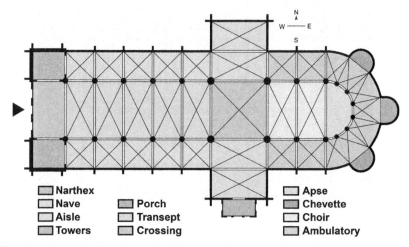

Generic schematic plan of a cathedral.

The Norman construction of Canterbury Cathedral was built from 1070-1077 on the site of the Anglo-Saxon cathedral that was destroyed by fire in 1067. A good portion of the Norman construction survives in the middle section of the cathedral: this part is 900 years old. Since then, Canterbury Cathedral has undergone four additional renovations (following fires) and additions. Here are some highlights of Canterbury Cathedral. First, note its size (above, see the tiny people walking in front). Notice also the many "statues" imbedded in the walls of the lower part of the cathedral walls. These are church fathers, literally and figuratively the "pillars" of the church. Next are the cathedral's famous stained glass windows. Sorry you will only see these in black and white (below).

Selection of Poor Man's Bible stain glass window in Canterbury Cathedral.
https://commons.wikimedia.org/wiki/
File:Canterbury_Cathedral_020_Poor_Mans_Bbible_Window_01_adj.JPG
See page for author [Public domain], via Wikimedia Commons

The stained glass windows are constructed in brilliant colors of reds, golds, greens, and a dazzling cobalt blue. From the inside they are brilliant with the sunlight shining through. From the outside they are colorless as you can see in the photo of the exterior above. This is another reminder that God's glory is available *inside* the cathedral, a sacred space. Outside, the world of the flesh lurks to tempt even the strong. Another highlight of Canterbury is its interior, designed again to reinforce the idea of God's magnificence and man's insignificance. Hopefully, you can get the idea of the cathedral's immense size, inside and out. Another breath-taking site is the altar at the East end (the apse) of the cathedral.

High altar of Canterbury Cathedral.
https://commons.wikimedia.org/wiki/File%3ACanterbury_Cathedral_Altar.jpg
By Skyden67 (Own work) [CC BY-SA 3.0 (http://creativecommons.org/licenses/by-sa/3.0)], via Wikimedia Commons

Can you venture a guess as to why the altar is placed at the East and the door to the outside world is placed at the West? Also notice the steps approaching the altar and the steps even beyond. This is the oldest part of the church Notice the

Romanesque arches (they are rounded). This part was built during the Norman building phases (1070-1077).

Nave of Canterbury Cathedral viewed from raised area of the rood screen separating the nave from the choir.

Many stories are connected to Canterbury Cathedral. Two of the most important are the martyrdom of Thomas à Becket, Archbishop of Canterbury, and Chaucer's *Canterbury Tales*. **Thomas à Becket** began his career as a friend and colleague of King Henry II of England, and when the Archbishop of Canterbury's position came open (the current Archbishop Theobald died in 1161), Henry appointed Thomas as Archbishop against Thomas' wishes. Henry hoped to receive approval from Thomas to gain control over the Church in England (at that time, all kings had to get permission from the Church to wage war, marry, make any alliances). Thomas refused to grant Henry the powers that he wished, and eventually four of Henry's knights murdered Thomas in the Cathedral on December 29, 1170.

Becket Altar in Canterbury Cathedral.
https://commons.wikimedia.org/wiki/File:Becket_Altar.JPG
By Angelsfan27000 (Own work) [Public domain], via Wikimedia Commons

Canterbury became an immediate pilgrimage destination for the faithful; it has lasted as a pilgrimage destination for 900 years. The modern sculpture of sword and cross marks the spot in the Cathedral where Becket was murdered. At the Cathedral's highest point, an eternal flame burns in his memory. Even in the twentieth century, T. S. Eliot, a famous American-British writer, wrote a play entitled *Murder in the Cathedral* (1935), dramatizing the murder of Becket by the four knights.

The other major "story" connected with Canterbury Cathedral is **Chaucer's *Canterbury Tales*** (1380-92). *Canterbury Tales* is rather a group of stories. The work's premise is that "pilgrims" on a pilgrimage to Canterbury Cathedral decide to make the time pass more pleasantly by recounting two tales each—one on the way to Canterbury and one on the way home. However, we never hear the tales told on the way home, just those going *to* Canterbury. The "pilgrims" represent a cross-section of people from all social classes including lawyers and the clergy—humanity in general. Most of the tales are gentle "satires" of various aspects of society. Chaucer even takes on the Church at a time when that could have resulted in being charged with heresy. However, he couched his satire in tales that seemed harmless, like the Nun's Priest's famous tale of Chanticleer and Pertelote, a pair of very well-read chickens. In the *Ellesmere Manuscripts* (housed at the Huntington Museum in California and the most pristine copy of *Canterbury Tales* in existence) each pilgrim has a woodcut, (an image cut into wood, then stamped on the vellum of the manuscript and colored). In the *Tales*, Chaucer represents himself as a pilgrim, who, the other pilgrims agree, tells a terrible tale.

Canterbury Cathedral tells its own story. In its walls and windows and archways and ceilings it tells tales that specifically glorify God and reveal in stone and glass God's word to the throngs of parishioners most of whom could not read or had no access to the *Bible* if they could. Thousands of tales reside *in* the Cathedral itself. Yet, many other stories have a connection with this very famous storytelling monument to God.

Stories of Man: The Renaissance in Europe

A major sea change occurred toward the end of the fourteenth century in Europe: The Renaissance. Remember the Byzantine Empire (the Eastern Roman Empire) talked about earlier? It flourished in Eastern Europe and parts of the Middle East all through the Middle Ages in Europe; the Byzantine Empire lasted almost 1500 years. However, the army of the Ottoman Empire invaded and captured Constantinople in 1453 marking the Byzantine Empire's end and dealing a massive blow to Christendom in the process. The Hagia Sophia in Constantinople (built 532-37 by Christian Emperor Justinian I), was the center for the Greek Orthodox Church; after the capture of Constantinople, it was converted into a mosque. Many Greeks and other intellectuals fled the city before and after the siege, with most of them migrating to Italy. This helped fuel the Renaissance because they brought with them many Greek and Roman manuscripts from the Byzantine libraries and began the "rebirth" of learning that marks the Renaissance in Europe.

Many other factors contributed to this process. The Church (there was only one Church in Europe and it corresponded to the Roman Catholic Church of today) was losing its control over the people; it had implemented an Inquisition to bring the sheep back into the fold. Some of the Inquisition's methods were cruel and barbaric and further alienated the people. In addition, many Church officials had become rich, powerful, and corrupt at the expense of the poor. The Crusades, too, had been in full force with the goal of retaking the Holy Land for the Church. These forays into the Middle East marked the beginning of European trade and exploration and curiosity about a world most never realized existed. Most importantly, around 1475 Gutenberg invented the Printing Press and opened the world of reading to the masses. Suddenly those who could read had books and those who couldn't read wanted to read. It was an intellectual and geographical explosion of ideas. And the focus began to shift from stories of God to stories of Man. *Humanism* was the name of the Renaissance game and Man (not God) was "the measure of all things." The whole idea is reflected in the art (Michelangelo and Leonardo Da Vinci), drama (Shakespeare), music (the madrigal on into opera), history (a rediscovery of the civilizations of Greece and Rome), Greek philosophy (Socrates, Plato, Aristotle), and religion (new translations of the Bible that no longer depended on St. Jerome's singular Latin translation).

Michelangelo's *David*.
https://commons.wikimedia.org/wiki/File%3AMichelangelo-David_JB01.JPG
By Jörg Bittner Unna (Own work) [CC BY 3.0 (http://creativecommons.org/licenses/by/3.0)], via Wikimedia Commons

Just one look at the magnificent sculpture above of **David** by **Michelangelo** (1504) explains a lot. What is man's place in the Renaissance? In Michelangelo's depiction, this "man" is larger than life: the statue is 14.2 feet tall, 17 feet with the base included. *David* is physically perfect. And he's made of marble. This is a statue of David, as in David and Goliath—the Bible story. David, a young Israeli shepherd boy, volunteers to fight Goliath, a giant of a man and a Philistine, with the agreement that whoever wins the battle will rule the other tribe. David goes against Goliath with only a slingshot and five pebbles but with God on his side. He defeats the giant. Does Michelangelo's David look like a young boy? The only similarity it seems is the slingshot over his shoulder. The Renaissance ideal was a perfect mind in a perfect body.

Leonardo da Vinci was another Renaissance artist obsessed with the accurate depiction of the idealized human body. Both he and Michelangelo illegally gained access to dead bodies so that they could dissect and understand the bodies (i.e., muscles, organs, bone structure) and properly represent the human form in their art. Leonardo has notebook after notebook of anatomical drawings precise enough to be the basis of any freshman level anatomy and physiology textbook today. And then, of course, is Leonardo's famous drawing of man showing his proportions precisely. The drawing below, pen and ink on paper and entitled **Vitruvian Man** (1490), depicts a man in two superimposed positions with his arms and legs apart and inscribed in both a circle and a square demonstrating man's ideal proportions. The texts above and below the drawing (in Leonardo's "mirrored handwriting") explain those proportions based on the work of architect Vitruvius, a Roman architect and civil engineer (ca. 80-15 BCE), and show the Renaissance fascination with the connections between art and science.

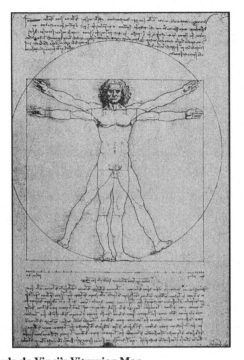

Leonardo da Vinci's Vitruvian Man.
https://commons.wikimedia.org/wiki/File%3AStudio_del_Corpo_Umano_-
_Leonardo_da_Vinci.png
Leonardo da Vinci [Public domain], via Wikimedia Commons

The Renaissance was a time of ferment and revolution — a revolution in the way people thought about the world. A religious revolution occurred when **Martin Luther** walked up to the door of the church in Wittenberg, Germany in 1517 and nailed to it his "95 Theses." These proclaimed the Bible as the central religious authority (not the Pope or the church officials) and asserted that individuals may reach salvation by their faith not by their deeds or confession to representatives of the Church. This act sparked the **Protestant Reformation**. This is why we have Protestant Churches (Lutheran, Anglican, Presbyterian, Methodist) today instead of just a single belief system, that of the Roman Catholic Church (it wasn't called the Roman Catholic Church then), that existed up until that point.

With the decline of the Church's power, the rise in intellectual curiosity, and access to great thinkers of the past, the Scientific Revolution began during this period. Yes, scientists tell stories too in the form of "theories" and "principles." The most famous scientific "storyteller" of the time was **Galileo**, an Italian astronomer, physicist, engineer, philosopher, and mathematician (1564-1642). His outstanding invention was the telescope; his first was made in 1609 and magnified objects three times; three years later, he had one made that could magnify objects twenty times. With this one, he was able to look at the moon, discover the four satellites of Jupiter, observe a supernova, verify the phases of Venus, and discover sunspots. Prior to this and for over 2000 years, it had been held that the sun revolved around the earth (Figure 1 below: Ptolemic System —from the Greek mathematician Ptolemy). The blob in the center represents earth. Before the Renaissance, the universe was considered "earth-centered." Galileo's discoveries proved the Copernican System (Figure 2 below): that the earth and other planets revolve around the sun—and in elliptical orbits (though the 500 year-old drawing below does not show that).

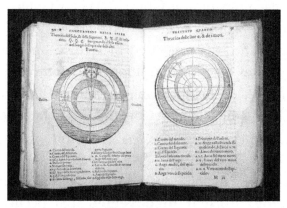

Fig. 1: Ptolemic System (earth-centered)
https://commons.wikimedia.org/wiki/File:1550_SACROBOSCO_Tractatus_de_Sphaera_-_(16)_Ex_Libris_rare_-_Mario_Taddei.JPG
By Mauro Fiorentino, Theosebo, Phonasco, & Philopanareto. [Public domain], via Wikimedia Commons

Fig. 2: Copernican System (sun-centered)
https://commons.wikimedia.org/wiki/File%3ADe_Revolutionibus_manuscript_p9b.jpg
By Nicolas Copernicus (www.bj.uj.edu.pl) [Public domain], via Wikimedia Commons

The idea of a sun-centered universe was extremely controversial and this scientific idea along with others—most notably Galileo's concept of the existence of gravity—went against the teachings of the Church. When Galileo published his most famous work, *Dialogue Concerning the Two Chief World Systems* in 1632, he was suspected of heresy (speaking against the Church), tried by the Inquisition, and sentenced to house arrest for the rest of his life. Galileo suffered for the story he told, but it had a huge impact on the scientific "stories" that came later, especially those of Newton, Einstein, and Heisenberg.

Even these "Revolutions" do not take into account the enormous **geographical discoveries** that occurred during this period: namely the discovery of an entirely "New World" that no one in Europe—NO ONE—knew was there. Columbus and his men were looking for a shorter trade route to India and

China when they bumped into what is now Cuba and the Dominican Republic. When Columbus set sail in 1491, many people still believed that the world was flat. Columbus could not possibly have known the impact the New World he found would have on the future of mankind. Following his discovery, the New World was partially explored by such notables as Balboa (discovered the Pacific Ocean at Panama, 1513), Ponce de Leon (Puerto Rico and Florida, 1508-11), Cortez (Mexico and the Aztec Empire, 1519-21), Pizarro (Peru, 1531-33), Cabot (looking for a Northwest Passage to Asian trade, 1497), Francis Drake (California, 1579), and Hudson (New York and Hudson River, 1609-11). Magellan and his men sailed around the world between 1519 and 1522). Australia and New Zealand were discovered in 1642-44, and trade routes to the East (Japan, India) were opened between 1542 and 1565.

Below are two maps. The first is a Map of the World ca. 1400 at the beginning of the Renaissance; the second is a Map of the World printed in 1570. The Renaissance was an Age of Discovery in every sense.

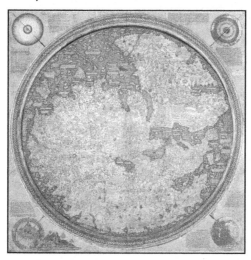

Map of the world, ca. 1400
https://commons.wikimedia.org/wiki/File:FraMauroDetailedMap.jpg
By Piero Falchetta ("The Fra Mauro map") [Public domain], via Wikimedia Commons

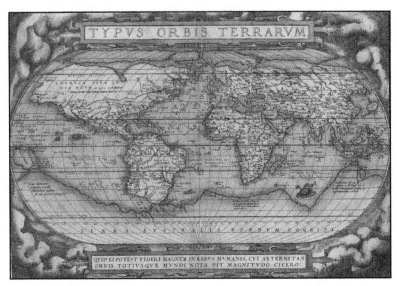

Map of the world, 1570

Part IV: War and Turbulence

Again, we are fast-forwarding from selected important stories of the Renaissance to the turbulent war-torn years of the Twentieth Century, a leap of almost four hundred years. Much happened, of course, in that time. Most importantly for us was the **American Revolution** (1776), the establishment of the United States of America, and the Westward Expansion of the country. We were not the only ones who revolted against our master. Other European countries followed suit, most notably the French. **The French Revolution** (1789-99) was waged against the extravagant lifestyle and spending of the monarchy King Louis XVI and his wife Marie-Antoinette who occupied the opulent Palace of Versailles. However, this revolution did not have the same effect as the American Revolution. **Napoleon** seized power in 1799 following The Reign of Terror between 1793-1794 led by a man named Robespierre (over 16,000 were put to death by the guillotine during that year), and set about to conquer the world.

And then, of course between about 1760 and 1840, another revolution took place, this one just as important as the rest: the **Industrial Revolution**. The Industrial Revolution marks the beginning of a new type of production that began with the invention of the steam engine by James Watt and led to other technological advancements. These inventions went on to power machinery, locomotives, and ships and ushered Europe (and America with it) into the Industrial Age. Though by our standards, technological progress of the Industrial Revolution may seem slow (it took over a century for its full effects to be felt), the Industrial Revolution ushered in a plethora of problems we have yet to solve: urbanization, the environmental impact of industry on nature, changes in social mores, the redistribution of wealth.

During this time period in America, we had our own crisis: we fought the only war ever fought on our soil: the **Civil War (1861-65).** Slavery was at the heart of the conflict, but even beyond that, the two factions were fighting to maintain their way of life: The South wanted to keep its agrarian economy based on tobacco, cotton, and other crops; the North wanted to move forward with industrialization. The South needed slaves (or thought they did) to maintain their economy; the North did not. Of course, slavery was a moral issue as well, one that went against the foundations of our country. Even though the North won and slavery was abolished, the repercussions of the slavery issue resurfaced in the Civil Rights movement of the 1960s and remains with us today.

The Twentieth Century saw the world that had existed for millennia coming apart at the seams, and no one knew quite what to do about it. No wonder it was so turbulent. The Twentieth Century marked another very dramatic change as well: war would not only involve one country against another; war would involve the countries of the *world*. This was a brand new phenomenon, one that had been faced at no other time in history. Human beings no longer lived in isolation, one town from another, one country from another. We found ourselves in a *global community* where what affected one country affected all. We were all in this together whether we wanted to be or not. An overview of the **century's major conflicts** include the following: World War I (1914-18); the Russian Revolution and Civil War (1917-21); the Spanish Civil War (1936-39); World War II (1939-45); the Cold War (1945-90); the Korean Conflict (1950-53—still unsettled); the Vietnam War (1959-73); the Antiwar and Civil Rights Movements in the U. S. (1960s); First Iraq War (1990-91).

The turbulence surfaced in the stories the Twentieth Century told. Even before the outbreak of World War II, we see it manifested in the arts, in **Stravinsky's** scandalous ballet, *Le Sacre du Printemps*: *The Rite of Spring.* No musical work has had such a powerful influence or evoked as much controversy as this ballet that premiered on May 29, 1913 at the Théatre des Champs-Elysées in Paris. According to NPR's "Performance Today: Milestone of the Millennium" (1999), in addition to its "outrageous costumes, unusual choreography and bizarre story of pagan sacrifice," Stravinsky's musical innovations tested the patience of the audience of the day. This audience was used to sedate classical ballets like *Swan Lake* (1877) that, like *The Rite of Spring*, had its impetus from Russian folk tales, but rewarded the audience's expectations with a graceful, lilting musical performance. Instead, the Paris premier of *The Rite of Spring* created a furor described by the NPR host as "angular, dissonant, and totally unpredictable." Dancing began to "loud, pulsating, dissonant cords with jarring, irregular accents." Instruments were used in bizarre ways and pushed to the extremes of their ranges; village dances were comprised of teams moving in seemingly random patterns, forming and reforming, creating pile-ups of sound and movement. To the audience, the result was sensory overload accompanied by raw, vital rhythms. They responded with hisses, catcalls, and yells so loud that the dancers couldn't hear the music or stay in sync. The ballet "redefined twentieth-century music" according to a PBS article on Stravinsky's *The Rite of Spring*. "You never know when or where revolutions will start," the article announces. "They can be social or political or artistic. Often, these artistic revolutions—revolutions in taste—seem to predict other changes in society."

Drawing of Marie Piltz in the "Sacrificial Dance" from The Rite of Spring.
https://en.wikipedia.org/wiki/File:Sacrificialdance.jpg
Published in Montjoie! (magazine), Paris, June 1913. Scanned from T.F. Kelly: First Nights: Five Musical Premieres. Yale University Press, New Haven 2000. ISBN 978-0-300-09105-2

Before the artistic scandal surrounding the ballet subsided, the world found itself embroiled in the **First World War (1914-18).** The total number of deaths of military and civilian casualties in World War I was over 37 million: 17 million dead and 20 million wounded, making it one of the deadliest conflicts in human history. At Verdun, the war's longest and most costly battle (February to December 1916), the most reliable estimates suggest the battle resulted in 700,000 casualties with over 300,000 men dead or missing. The Allies in World War I were Great Britain, France, Russia, Italy, and finally the U. S.; the Central Powers were Germany, the Austrian-Hungarian Empire, the Ottoman Empire, and Bulgaria. Meanwhile in Russia, the Bolshevik Revolution occurred in 1917. The Bolsheviks, or workers, dismantled the Tsarist autocracy and replaced it with a Communist government. A civil war ensued and lasted for several years between the "Reds" (Bolsheviks), the "Whites" (anti-socialists), and the non-Boshevik socialists. Finally, in 1922, the Union of Soviet Socialist Republics (USSR—the "Soviet Union") was created.

Stravinky's *The Rite of Spring* ushered in the turbulent twentieth century with a vengeance.

Woodrow Wilson, the U. S. President from 1913 to 1921, managed to keep America out of the war until 1917 when two battles (Verdun was one) resulted in over a half million casualties each. Wilson told the American people and the world that the war would "make the world safe for democracy" and that it would be a "war to end war." He was wrong. By 1933, Adolf Hitler had been elected Chancellor of Germany and by 1936, the **Spanish Civil War**, World War II's harbinger, was underway. The Nationalists, as the Spanish military rebels called themselves, were supported by Fascist Italy and Nazi Germany. The Republican government against whom the Nationalists revolted, were supported by the Soviet Union and volunteers from Europe and the United States. The nations of the world had once again aligned. A defining moment came on April 26, 1937. The Basque town of **Guernica** in Spain suffered an aerial attack carried out *for* the Spanish nationalist government *by* its allies, the Germans and the Italians. Guernica was a rehearsal for World War II. German air chief Hermann Göering testified at his trial following World War II that "The Spanish Civil War gave me an opportunity to put my young air force to the test, and a means for my men to gain experience." (Eyewitness to History.com). Guernica became an everlasting symbol of the atrocities of war. Its people were guinea pigs in a German military experiment.

Ruins of Guernica after Nazi bombing.
https://commons.wikimedia.org/wiki/File:Bundesarchiv_Bild_183-
H25224%2C_Guernica%2C_Ruinen.jpg
Bundesarchiv, Bild 183-H25224 / Unknown / CC-BY-SA 3.0 [CC BY-SA 3.0 de (http://creativecommons.org/licenses/by-sa/3.0/de/deed.en)], via Wikimedia Commons

Guernica also became the impetus for one of the most famous paintings of the twentieth century, ***Guernica* by Pablo Picasso** (1937); the painting remains a "story" of the wars and turbulence of the twentieth century, perhaps a "story" of the wars and turbulence of all time. This is Picasso's most famous work, and it is monumental, measuring 11 feet tall and 25.6 feet wide. (Wiki image can be found at: https://en.wikipedia.org/wiki/File:PicassoGuernica.jpg) Picasso himself was Spanish and he had been commissioned by the Spanish Republican government to exhibit a piece for the Paris Exhibition to be held in the summer of 1937. After the bombing, he deserted his original idea and began the *Guernica*; it took him a little over a month to complete. The initial reaction to the painting was critical, especially by the Germans who called it "a hodgepodge of body parts that any four-year-old could have painted." However, it became over the years an emblem of the destruction of war and its human cost. Painted in shades of grey, black, white, and blue, it makes use both of Picasso's cubist style in which the painter analyzed natural forms and reduced them to basic geometric parts on a two-dimensional plane. The work also utilizes some of Picasso's most recurring symbols: the bull (or minotaur) and the horse coupled with his anatomical disjointed figures and body parts reminiscent of the bodies in some of his earlier paintings. Also suggested is the influence of the primitive (especially African masks) evident in his earlier styles. Both the mask and disjoined figures are evident in this painting of 1907, *Les Demoiselles d'Avignon*.

Les Demoiselles d'Avignon **by Picasso.**
https://en.wikipedia.org/wiki/File:Les_Demoiselles_d%27Avignon.jpg
Pablo Picasso completed *Les Demoiselles d'Avignon* in 1907. Les Demoiselles d'Avignon appeared in the May 1910 edition of the Architectural Record, a US publication.
[Public domain], via Wikimedia Commons

By now the connection between the turbulence of the twentieth century and the expressions of it in music/dance (Stravinsky's *The Rite of Spring*) and Picasso's paintings, both early (*Les Demoiselles d'Avignon*) and mid-career (*Guernica*) should be surfacing.

On September 1939, only two years after the bombing of Guernica and the exhibition of Picasso's painting, **Adolf Hitler** invaded Poland, an event that marked the beginning of World War II and pitted the Axis Powers (Germany, Italy, and Japan) against the Allies (the U. S., Great Britain, France). One might ask how this happened: How did Hitler manage to get elected Chancellor of Germany in 1933 and gain such power that by 1939, he could march 1.5 million troops across the 1,750 mile border of Poland claiming his massive invasion was a defensive action?

The answer: Hitler was the Twentieth Century's most effective storyteller.

Before we get to the story Hitler told the German people, we need to look at least one study by psychologists Melanie Green and Timothy Brock (2004). Their findings, highlighted in *The Storytelling Animal* by Jonathan Gottschall (2014) suggest that the more absorbed readers become in a story, the more the story alters their beliefs. "Highly absorbed readers," Gottschall maintains, detect "significantly fewer 'false notes' in stories" than less absorbed listeners or readers. When we read nonfiction, Gottschall suggests, we tend to be "critical and skeptical," but when we are "absorbed in a story, we drop our intellectual guard." Being moved emotionally seems to leave us defenseless. This makes storytelling a very powerful tool indeed, one that can "change the world" for good or ill.

Hitler was an expert storyteller. And, at least in part, he was influenced by his intense passion for the humanities, especially visual art and music. He was especially drawn to the music of **Richard Wagner**. Wagner (1813-1883) was a German composer, famous for his operas and also for his anti-semitic writings. According to Hitler's childhood friend, August Kubizek, Hitler's epiphany came when, as young men, the two of them attended a performance of Richard Wagner's *Rienzi*, a political opera set in imperial Rome. Hitler believed the opera had revealed his destiny: to lead the German people "out of servitude to the heights of freedom." Hitler admits as much in *Mein Kampf* (*My Struggle*, his autobiography). "It began at that hour," he confesses in the book. Hitler, who considered Wagner a great revolutionary, said, "Whoever wants to understand National Socialist Germany must know Wagner." Most historians acknowledge the debt Hitler owed to Wagner, both in Wagner's operatic heroes (especially Parsifal and Siegfried) and in his anti-Semitic writings that included "Judaism in Music" and "Hero-dom and Christendom" (Rosefield's article, historytoday.com). According to Jonathan Gottschall, Hitler "believed himself to be a Wagnerian hero": Lohengrin, Siegfried and "especially Parsifal . . . a modern knight locked in a struggle with evil."

Hitler joined the **Nazi Party** in 1919. The Nazi Party was anti-Marxist (and therefore anti-Russian) and opposed to the democratic post-World War II governments; it advocated extreme nationalism (extreme loyalty to the German nation) and anti-Semitism. Hitler rose to a place of prominence during the Nazi party's early years as a speaker and an organizer, and was willing to use violence to advance his agenda. His attempt at a *coup* (overthrow of the government) in Bavaria, his arrest and imprisonment, and the publication of his book, *Mein Kampf,* gave him a platform to publicize his nationalist sentiment to the nation. The Wall Street Crash of 1929 ushered in worldwide economic disaster allowing the Nazis to make great gains in the German political structure and struck a blow against democracy. From 1931-1933, the Nazis combined terror tactics with conventional campaigning as Hitler evoked support with his powerful speeches even as his troops paraded in the streets, beat up opponents, and broke up meetings. Such tactics continued until in July of 1932; the Nazi party gained almost 14,000,000 votes.

Nürnberg Rally of Nazi Party, 1934.

By January 1933, Hitler was made Chancellor of Germany. "I tell you," Hitler declared to a British correspondent in Berlin in 1934, "the National Socialist movement will go on for 1,000 years! . . . Don't forget how people laughed at me 15 years ago when I declared that one day I would govern Germany. They laugh now, just as foolishly, when I declare that I shall remain in power!"

Basically Hitler had a story: the German people, defeated by the Allied Powers in World War I and now economically exhausted and deprived, deserved their dignity, the dignity commanded by their Germanic heroes and he,

Hitler, was one. He rehearsed his story and methodically brought it to the masses via cheap radios, factory concerts and mobile village cinemas organized through the Propaganda Ministry under its Minister, Paul Joseph Goebbels.

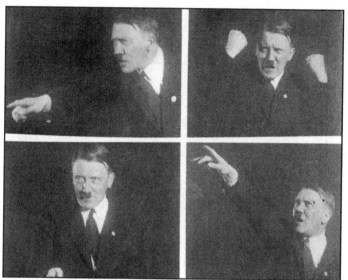

Speech rehearsals and poses of Adolf Hitler, leader of the Nazi Party.
https://commons.wikimedia.org/wiki/File:Bundesarchiv_Bild_102-10460%2C_Adolf_Hitler%2C_Rednerposen.jpg
Bundesarchiv, Bild 102-10460 / Hoffmann, Heinrich / CC-BY-SA [CC BY-SA 3.0 de (http://creativecommons.org/licenses/by-sa/3.0/de/deed.en)], via Wikimedia Commons

Hitler and Goebbels were masters of **propaganda** (biased or misleading information used to promote or publicize a particular political cause or point of view). They were both master storytellers, playing upon the emotions of their audience, the German people, for support. Hitler held massive parades and huge rallies, such as the Youth Rally at Nuremberg in 1935 attended by over one million. According to Aldous Huxley in his 1958 essay "Propaganda Under a Dictatorship," Hitler differed "from all his predecessors in history" in that he "made complete use of all technical means" to tell his story for the purpose of dominating his country and conquering the world. Hitler's Propaganda Ministry burned books that were considered "un-German in spirit"—those written by Jews, modernists, socialists, "art-Bolsheviks"—any writing considered hostile or damaging to the Nazi Party.

Book burning rally in Berlin, May, 1933.

Hitler completely understood the power of the story to transport his audience, the power of the narrative to *modify people's deepest moral beliefs and values*, and the power of fiction to sculpt individuals and societies. This is certainly a lesson to be learned through studying the humanities.

Hitler's storytelling tactics almost enabled him to conquer the world. It led him to put to death in the most brutal ways possible six million Jews, perhaps in some cases to Wagner's music.

The outcome of World War II, however, was influenced by the scientific "stories" told by two individuals decades before World War II: Albert Einstein and Werner Heisenberg. In the world of science, these "stories" are called "theories" or "principles."

Albert Einstein shook the foundations of physics with the publication of his *Special Theory of Relativity* in 1905 and his *General Theory of Relativity* in 1915. By the time these papers were published, three hundred years had passed since Galileo's "stories" of gravity. During this time, many scientists continued trying to explain the physical world. The most notable of these was **Isaac Newton** (1643-1727) who, in his *Principia* published in 1687, put forth his Three Laws of Motion: 1) Every object in a state of uniform motion tends to remain in that state unless an external force is applied; 2) *F=ma* : the *force* of an object is equal to *mass* times *acceleration*; 3) For every action there is an equal and opposite reaction. Newton's law of universal gravitation is another scientific "story" (image at below) that states that any two bodies in the universe attract each other with a force called gravity.

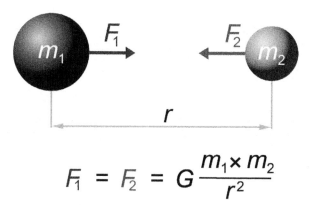

$$F_1 = F_2 = G \frac{m_1 \times m_2}{r^2}$$

Newton's mathematical equation of the Law of Universal Gravity.
https://commons.wikimedia.org/wiki/File:NewtonsLawOfUniversalGravitation.svg
I, Dennis Nilsson [CC BY 3.0 (http://creativecommons.org/licenses/by/3.0)], via Wikimedia Commons

In order for Newton to tell his scientific "stories," he had to invent a brand new language: calculus, a branch of mathematics that deals with rates of change. Ever since then, Newton's principles have served to explain the workings of the visible world as well as the movements of planet and stars.

However, **Einstein's Special Theory of Relativity** (1905) showed that Newton's Three Laws of Motion were only approximately correct and began to break down when velocities approached the speed of light. $E=mc^2$ is probably the most famous equation in history. It came out of Einstein's "story" about "special relativity," a radical new way to explain the motions of objects in the universe. The equation means *energy* (E) in a system is equal to its total *mass* (m) multiplied by the square of the speed of light (c^2), a constant (c=186,000 miles per second). Einstein determined that the speed of light is constant and that nothing can travel faster. He also suggested that mass can change to energy and back to mass again which meant that mass and energy are just different aspects of the same thing. This is what enables the release of a huge amount of energy produce a nuclear explosion. Nuclear power stations exploit this idea inside their reactors wherein neutrons split the nuclei of uranium atoms producing *fission*, a release of energy that results in a chain reaction of atom-splitting. This principle can be used to produce power for cities, but it is also responsible for fission, the principle behind the creation of the atomic bomb.

Einstein also determined that there is no fixed frame of reference in the universe; events look different depending on where the observer is in relation to the event. This is where the idea of "relativity" comes in. We all see events differently depending on where we are when we observe them. In his 1915 paper on the **General Theory of Relativity** Einstein introduced a phenomenon he called *time dilation* which means that time does not pass at the same rate for everyone. A fast-moving observer measures time passing more slowly than a (relatively) stationary observer would. In other words, a moving clock runs more slowly than a stationary one (see earth and spaceship below). Also, a fast-moving object appears shorter along the direction of motion relative to a slow-moving object; the effect is very subtle until the object travels close to the speed of light.

Depiction of time dilation of person on earth and person moving at the speed of light.
http://cnx.org/contents/d6555a80-80d8-4829-9346-07ea9391f391@5/
Simultaneity_And_Time_Dilation
© Nov 5, 2012 OpenStax College
Download for free at http://cnx.org/contents/d6555a80-80d8-4829-9346-07ea9391f391@5.

Moreover, space and time are part of one continuum, called *space-time*. Time is the fourth dimension. Space-time can be thought of as a grid of fabric. The presence of mass distorts space-time, so the rubber sheet model is a popular visualization (see following image).

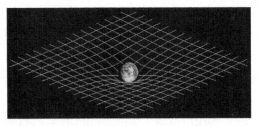

Space-time curvature.
https://commons.wikimedia.org/wiki/File:Spacetime_curvature.png#file
Created by User:Johnstone using a 3D CAD software package and an image of planet earth
from NASA's Galileo spacecraft.

Gravity also bends light, a phenomenon called *gravitational lensing*. When we observe a distant galaxy, the gravity of matter between Earth and the galaxy causes light rays to be bent into different paths (see image below). When the light reaches the telescope, sometimes multiple images of the same star or galaxy appear.

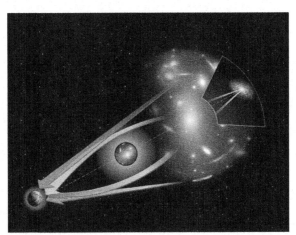

Gravitational lensing.
https://commons.wikimedia.org/wiki/File:Gravitational_lens-full.jpg
Material credited to STScI on this site was created, authored, and/or prepared for NASA
under Contract NAS5-26555. Unless otherwise specifically stated, no claim to copyright is
being asserted by STScI and it may be freely used as in the public domain in accordance with
NASA's contract.

The bottom line is, thanks to Einstein, we will never see the world in the same way again. Everything in the universe is "relative" to everything else. We see this especially in the art of the time, Picasso's *Les Demoiselles d'Avignon* and *Guernica*, for example, where shapes are warped by the artist in order to demonstrate this "relative" way of viewing the world calling into question even the way we see.

While Albert Einstein's "stories"—his theories—refined and expanded Newton's laws dealing with the physical world on a large scale (the physical world we can see), **Werner Heisenberg** (1901-76) is credited with formulating the **Uncertainty Principle** behind quantum mechanics, a "story"—a principle—that attempts to explain the behavior of matter and energy in atoms and subatomic particles. According to Heisenberg's Principle, it is not possible to measure (i.e. to magnify to the classical level) both the *position* and the *momentum* of a particle accurately at the same time. The more accurately the position of a particle is measured, the less accurately we can measure its momentum and vice versa.

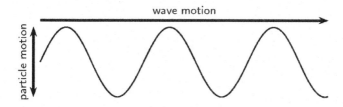

Particle-Wave phenomenon.
© Feb 23, 2012 Free High School Science Texts Project
http://cnx.org/contents/dfe0228f-b99c-46e0-ab4e-19945ec83d97@7.2:20/
Siyavula_textbooks:_Grade_10_P
Download for free at http://cnx.org/contents/dfe0228f-b99c-46e0-ab4e-19945ec83d97@7.2.

Not only that, but the *Uncertainty Principle* calls into question the "reality" of a particle's very existence. This is because particles of both light and matter can display characteristics of both a wave and a particle. Waves have crests, troughs, and wavelengths; particles are a tiny packets of matter. In the famous "Dual-slit Experiment," this principle has been demonstrated many times over, proving the mysterious ways matter behaves at the subatomic level. In this experiment, photons of light are beamed at a screen with two narrow adjacent slits, and the image of light that passes through is observed on a second screen. The result is dark and light regions, called "interference fringes," build up. At first, it seems that the photons interfere with each other, but when the firing of the photon slowed down, it becomes clear that this is not what happens; what does happen is that we see that the photons are interacting with themselves within their own wave packet to produce the interference.

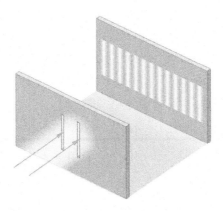

Dual-slit experiment.

When slowed even farther, we see that in some strange way each photon is interfering with itself. Its wave nature is interfering with its own wave. The same is true if electrons (particles of matter) are fired at the screen rather than photons.

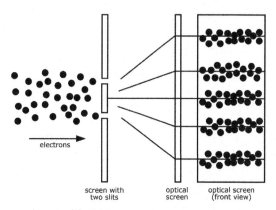

Dual-slit experiment with electrons.
https://commons.wikimedia.org/wiki/File%3ATwo-Slit_Experiment_Electrons.svg
By inductiveload (Own work (Own drawing)) [Public domain], via Wikimedia Commons

The conclusion: we must give up the idea of a photon or an electron having a specific location. The location of a subatomic particle is not defined until it is observed (such as striking a screen). The very act of measuring the position of a photon or electron disturbs the energy and position of subatomic particles.

These scientific "stories" were told almost a hundred years ago. In the scientific world they are called "theories"— *Einstein's theories of Special and General Relativity*—and "principles"—*Heisenberg's Uncertainty Principle*. Even if you've never heard of them, both have affected the way you and others see the world. After the Theories of Relativity and the Uncertainty Principle, our ideas of permanence and reality changed. No longer can we believe that what we see is "real" or concrete. We understand now that that which seems solid is just a collection of subatomic particles jiggling around each other, interfering with each other in ways we don't understand. Even the scientists can't agree. Every new observation raises new more complicated questions. Einstein himself was unhappy about the apparent randomness in nature that quantum mechanics suggested for the subatomic world. His famous phrase "God does not play dice" suggests that Heisenberg's "uncertainty" is only provisional; Einstein proposed that an underlying reality would be discovered in the future reconciling the visible world explained by Newton's Law and his own theories of relativity and the uncertainty associated with the subatomic particles of quantum mechanics. Such reconciliation would produce a Theory of Everything, a "story" that explains the universal realms, both large and small.

So far this hasn't happened. Einstein's theories of Relativity and Heisenberg's Uncertainty Principle ushered in an age in which we as human beings are less certain than we were in the past of our place—especially our individual places—in the scheme of things. This uncertainty was anticipated by Stravinsky's *The Rite of Spring* (1913) and Picasso's *Les Demoiselles d'Avignon* (1907), both of which were created before either Einstein or Heisenberg published their findings, before the First World War, and before the making of the atomic bomb, the first human invention with the capacity to destroy the world as we know it.

The humanities—art, music, dance, religion, literature, and philosophy—not only reflect but shape the emotional, psychic, and spiritual temper of the culture and times in which they are produced.

Part V: Freedom, Independence, and Possibility

In many ways, the forming of the United States of America is the telling of a new story, one that had never been told before. Think about it. The explorers of Europe, in an effort to find a trade route to the East (China, India), bumped into a brand new world that no one (except the Natives who had made the trek across the Bering Strait 12,000 years before) knew existed. The discovery the Europeans made had, of course, a two-fold impact: it displaced, and in many cases devastated, the native tribes that inhabited both North and South America; it captured the imaginations of the Renaissance Europe and its explorers and all of those who followed them.

The story of America has shaped us as a people and has shaped the stories we have told. The natives themselves who first settled what is now the United States fashioned our respect for nature and our sense that we must care for our land, our planet, if we are to ensure the future of our species. The Europeans who first settled North America in the 1600s brought with them a hope for religious freedom, a spirit of adventure and self-reliance, true grit in the wake of hardship. These people persevered and carved out an existence in a new land that offered promise and possibility. They valued education. They imported slaves. They established thirteen British colonies and rules to govern them with a population of 275,000 Anglos by 1700. Even so, the French and the Spanish vied with the British for the control of this new land. Here's what North America looked like around 1750 (see below).

Colonial settlement of North America around 1750.
https://commons.wikimedia.org/wiki/File:New-France1750.png
I, JF Lepage [GFDL (http://www.gnu.org/copyleft/fdl.html), CC-BY-SA-3.0 (http://
creativecommons.org/licenses/by-sa/3.0/), CC BY-SA 2.5-2.0-1.0 (http://
creativecommons.org/licenses/by-sa/2.5-2.0-1.0) or GFDL (http://www.gnu.org/copyleft/
fdl.html)], via Wikimedia Commons

By 1750, the New World, at least in North America, was in a tumultuous state. Slavery had a strong hold in the Southern colonies; even so, the South had experienced a number of violent uprisings from the slaves they possessed. In an effort to increase their political and economic power, the British and the French were locked in competition to acquire land in America, often displacing and/or alienating native tribes. The competition came to a head over the Ohio territory, and by 1754, the British colonists found themselves embroiled in the French and Indian War. In 1756, the British formally declared war on France, an act that distracted the British in dealing with colonial issues. The French and Indian War in some ways became a deciding factor in the Colonists' eventual revolt against the British.

Eventually, the colonists banded together and passed a series of "Acts" in protest against the British practice of taxing the colonies without allowing them to have representation in the British Parliament. This protest came to a head in 1773 with the Boston Tea Party: the colonists dumped an entire shipment of British East India Company tea into the Boston Harbor and precipitated the **American Revolution**. The colonists' fierce demand for independence from England took the form of several Continental Congresses, a number of battles (the Battle of Bunker Hill), and George Washington's becoming Commander of the Continental Army. Finally, on July 4, 1776, the Declaration of Independence was signed and the Revolutionary War for American independence from British rule began. The war lasted until 1783 when a peace treaty was finally signed and in 1787, the United States Constitution was ratified by the states. To the colonists and the rest of the world, it was a David and Goliath story re-enacted: David, in the form of a ragtag Colonial Army had won independence from Goliath, Great Britain, one of the most power nations in the world.

Our fierce championing of independence, our empathy for the underdog comes from our own struggle to be free of British control. The assertions set down in our Declaration of Independence are those we fiercely protect today: "that all men are created equal, that they are endowed by their Creator with certain unalienable Rights, that among these are Life, Liberty and the pursuit of Happiness." The Constitutional Amendments we protect as well: freedom of religion, freedom of speech, freedom to keep and bear arms, freedom from search and seizure or having to quarter soldiers in homes, the right to a speedy public trial by jury, the right to vote not based on race or sex—essentially, the freedom and the right to pursue our own destinies, to write our own stories. These beliefs are part of the American story and have shaped us all as American citizens.

In every respect, the American story is **The Great Experiment**. Unlike any other nation on earth up to 1776, we had a brand new start—no tribal squabbles, no national conflicts with the neighboring countries, no conquests and re-conquests over millennium as had occurred in the rest of the world. This is a big deal and it formed the basis for our idealism as a country. We felt after gaining our independence from Great Britain—and still feel today—that we are invincible. We feel that way even if common sense tells us otherwise.

Other people from other countries have bought into America's story as well, for we are a nation of immigrants. Most of those who immigrated during the Colonial Period (1600-1775) were from England, Germany, and the Scandinavian countries with some coming from Scotland and Ireland. During that period the Spanish also had a great impact on settling Mexico and Texas, and the French settled in what is now Canada and the Northeast. From the birth of our nation in 1783 through 1840 nearly all the population growth was by internal increase. That means that not many immigrants came to the U.S. during that period. However, the land the United States possessed increased dramatically. **The Louisiana Purchase**, bought by the far-sighted President Thomas Jefferson from Napoleon for $15 million in 1803, almost doubled the territory of the United States. The map below shows not only the size of the Louisiana Purchase, but the way the United States expanded in the 1800s.

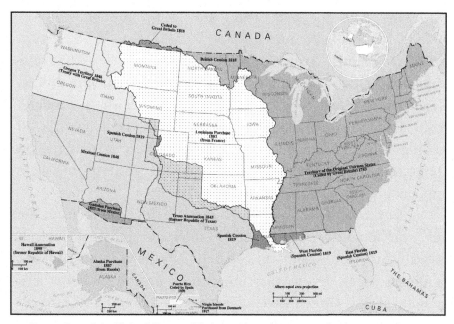

Expansion of the United States with dates of territories acquired.
https://commons.wikimedia.org/wiki/File:UnitedStatesExpansion.png
By The United States government (National Atlas of the United States) [Public domain], via
Wikimedia Commons

The exploration of **Lewis and Clark** (1803-04) awakened American's adventurous spirit, opened the way for the westward movement, and brought forth the notion of **"Manifest Destiny,"** which encapsulated the idea that America was "destined" to occupy the continent from coast to coast. This has been a part of our romantic notion of ourselves ever since. Even now, when all the land has been conquered and occupied, it's still a factor in our American psyche and part of our American story—in our art, our fiction, our songs. We still have more "space" for our citizens than almost any other country in the world. That's why we have bigger houses and bigger yards: we are, in relation to the rest of the world, still a *very* young country—barely reaching puberty by global standards.

In 1849, the California Gold Rush brought in over 100,000 would-be miners from the eastern U. S., Latin America, China, Australia, and Europe and by 1850 the immigration flood began. Between 1850 and 1930, 5 million Germans migrated to the US, 3.5 million British, 4.5 million Irish. Twenty-five million Europeans made the long trip, all seeking the America Dream of possibility ("Immigration Demographics"). By 1924 immigration restrictions were implemented and limits set.

Interrupting this all, of course, was the **Civil War**, the only war fought on American soil after our Independence. It lasted from 1861-1865 and pitted Northern states against Southern states. Up to that time, the northern and southern sections of the United States developed differently. The South remained predominantly agrarian while the North became industrialized. Because of this, different social cultures and political beliefs developed causing disagreements on issues such as taxes, tariffs, and states' rights—issues we are still debating today.

Of course, the central issue that led to the disruption of the Union was the debate over the future of slavery. That dispute led to secession by the South from the United States, and secession brought about a war in which the northern and western states and territories fought to preserve the Union, and the South fought to establish Southern independence as the Confederacy. As the war began, some 4 million Africans and their descendants toiled as slaves in the South. Owning slaves bestowed social position on their owners, and the slave ownership represented the largest portion of the South's personal and corporate wealth as cotton and land prices declined and the price of slaves soared. The country was divided (see map) and the country suffered the largest number of deaths of any other American conflict: 620,000 lost their lives. In the map below dark gray represents the Union states, stripes the Southern states, white the "border" states that permitted slavery, and light gray represents the territories at the time.

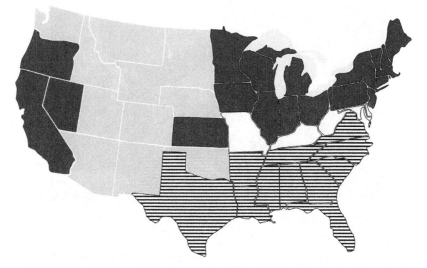

Anti-slave (dark gray), slave (striped) and "border" (white) states at the beginning of the Civil War, 1861.
https://commons.wikimedia.org/wiki/File:US_map_1864_Civil_War_divisions.svg
By Júlio Reis (by myself) [CC BY-SA 3.0 (http://creativecommons.org/licenses/by-sa/3.0)], via Wikimedia Commons. State colors adapted for black and white print.

With the end of the Civil War, slavery was abolished and the Union preserved. However, the fall out from the slavery issue remained. Slaves were freed but many remained indentured to their former masters having no skills, no education, and no means of supporting themselves. It took a hundred years for these issues to resurface, and resurface it did in the 1960s with the **Civil Rights Movement**. The movement polarized around another very astute storyteller, **Martin Luther King, Jr**. Martin Luther King, Jr. (1929-68) was a Baptist minister and a civil rights activist. During his years as a preacher, King had honed his ability to tell a story, and the story he told to whites and African Americans alike polarized the movement.

Martin Luther King, Jr. on steps of Lincoln Memorial, August, 1963.
https://de.wikipedia.org/wiki/Datei:USMC-09611.jpg#file
28. August 1963
http://www.marines.mil/unit/mcasiwakuni/PublishingImages/2010/01/KingPhoto.jpg
This image is a work of a U.S. military or Department of Defense employee, taken or made as part of that person's official duties. As a work of the U.S. federal government, the image is in the public domain.

His storytelling abilities enabled him to mobilize non-violent protests (that sometimes turned violent) and led to the Civil Rights Act of 1964 and the Voting Rights Act of 1965 and won King the Nobel Peace Prize in 1964. On Aug. 28, 1963, Martin Luther King led the March on Washington for Jobs and Freedom with approximately 250,000 attending (photo above). Here he delivered his "I Have A Dream" speech that remains the shining example of King's ability to tell a story that changed people's behavior.

Entangled with the Civil Rights Movement was the Vietnam War Protest Movement. Both took place in the 1960s and both evoked high levels of emotion that often resulted in violence. America entered the Vietnam War in 1961 by sending military and economic aid to South Vietnam and began air raids on North Vietnam and Communist-controlled areas in the south. The military draft was re-instated (this means men were called to serve in the army as they were in World Wars I and II), and by 1966, the U. S. had 190,000 troops in South Vietnam. Russia and China were supporting the North Vietnamese, the enemy of the South. In 1968, President Lyndon Johnson decided not to seek re-election citing the War in Vietnam as a factor. The length of the war, the high number of U. S. casualties (over 58,000 killed) and the U. S. involvement in the massacre at My Lai led to America's decision to withdraw.

The **Vietnam War** was not a popular one because of the story told to the American people by the news media that delivered its story via television. This was in high contrast to the news treatment of World War II when soldiers were glorified by radio and by government film footage on newsreels shown at movie theaters before feature films. Of course, the United States in World War II was engaged in a world war and had been attacked by the Japanese at Pearl Harbor. America was literally fighting for its way of life against the Germans led by Hitler, and against Italy and the Japanese. By contrast, during the Vietnam War, our troops were fighting a war in a tiny country that Americans had been told by its government was necessary in order to preserve our democratic way of life. This was the Government's story. It was governmental propaganda to gain support for the war. However, news reporters went to Vietnam and reported the news independently of the government, exposing the horrors of war to Americans gathered each evening around their TVs. Americans witnessed the "Casualty Reports" and became aware that their own soldiers often did not act heroically (the My Lai massacre, for example); they began to believe that the real reason for America's entry into the war was to fill the coffers of the military-industrial complex. The lack of support for the war led to our withdrawal in 1973 and the Communist takeover of Vietnam. One reason the Vietnam War became so controversial: the competing stories told by the Government on the one hand and the news media on the other. Storytelling is indeed a powerful force.

Student Vietnam War protesters at University of Wisconsin-Madison, January, 1965.
https://commons.wikimedia.org/wiki/File:Student_Vietnam_War_protesters.JPG
By uwdigitalcollections (Student protesters marching down Langdon Street) [CC BY 2.0 (http://creativecommons.org/licenses/by/2.0)], via Wikimedia Commons

The 1960s was a decade of social upheaval as illustrated by the Civil Rights Movement and the protests against the Vietnam War. It was also a decade of assassinations. **President John F. Kennedy** was assassinated in 1963; **Malcolm X**, a militant civil rights leader, in 1965; **Martin Luther King Jr.** and **Robert Kennedy** in 1968. To many it seemed that the world was falling apart, that anarchy had been unleashed, at least in this country.

During the last part of the century, the upheaval shifted away from domestic unrest in America to foreign shores. Iran seized U.S. hostages in 1980, and the Soviets invaded Afghanistan. And then, in 1990-91, the United States (with its coalition forces) invaded Iraq and launched **"Desert Storm,"** the First Gulf War. It proved a prelude to the September 11, 2001 attack on America and to America's subsequent retaliation in the Second Gulf War (2002).

Embedded in this briefest history of America are two stories that also tell America's story as a nation and our own as individuals. Both are stories of struggle, freedom, independence, and possibility. Both strike a cord deep within our human psyche probably because fiction seems to touch people's deepest moral beliefs and values. And these two stories have changed generations of readers and viewers and will probably continue to do so. These stories are *The Adventures of Huckleberry Finn* by Mark Twain and *Star Wars* by George Lucas.

Mark Twain is one of the great storytellers of all time. He was born in Missouri in 1835 as Samuel Clemens but wrote under the pen name, Mark Twain, a name taken from his few years piloting a steamboat on the Mississippi River. Hannibal, Missouri on the Mississippi River where Clemens grew up, furnishes the backdrop and basis of the fictionalized setting for ***The Adventures of Huckleberry Finn***, published in 1885. Since its publication, however, it has created much controversy. The novel is narrated by an outcast white boy, Huck, who helps his adult friend, a runaway slave named Jim, flee Missouri on a raft down the Mississippi River in the 1840s (pre-Civil War setting). Huck is a free-spirited and not always truthful hero who lacks respect for both religion and adult authority. This drew immediate fire from newspaper critics. Upon its publication, many called the book "tawdry" and its narrative voice (Huck's) "coarse" and "ignorant." The Concord, Massachusetts library banned it, labeling it as "trash and suitable only for the slums." However, many decades later, Nobel Prize Winner Ernest Hemingway claimed that "All modern American literature comes from one book by Mark Twain called *Huckleberry Finn*," and contemporary critics and scholars recognize it as one of the greatest American works of art.

Drawing of Huckleberry Finn by E.W. Kemble from the original 1884 edition.
https://commons.wikimedia.org/wiki/File:Huckleberry-finn-with-rabbit.jpg
By Edward Winsor Kemble (Transferred from en.wikipedia to Commons.) [Public domain], via Wikimedia Commons

Most consider Twain's satire to be a powerful attack on racism. Not everyone, of course, agrees. Some see it as inherently racist, mainly because of the repeated use of the word "nigger," a term used for slaves, especially in the 1840s, the time period in which the story is set. Over the 130 years the book has been in print, it as been banned and reinstated and banned and reinstated in libraries and school curricula many times over. It's the fourth most banned book in U. S. schools, so it must strike a chord. As recently as 2011 a new edition published by NewSouth Books has replaced the word "nigger" (used 219 times) with the word "slave" and the term "injun" with "Indian," again garnering much controversy. Dr. Sarah Churchwell, a lecturer on American literature, explained to the BBC in response to this new edition that changing the words makes a mockery of the story. "It's about a boy growing up a racist in a racist society who learns to reject that racism," she says. *Huckleberry Finn* seems to hit us Americans at the center of our core values and cause us to question them.

The second story, **Star Wars** by **George Lucas**, is a story still in progress. It is told through an American epic film series, a space opera that goes to the heart of the mythical hero tale. It began with the 1977 release of *Episode IV: The New Hope,* called then simply *Star Wars.* The events of the epic take place in a fictional galaxy full of alien creatures and robotic droids. Many planets are members of the Galactic Empire. The "Force" is an omnipresent energy harnessed only by those with the ability; it seems to be an energy field that surrounds all living things binding them together. The ability to harness it can be improved through training. The "Force" can be used for good, but has its "Dark Side" as well. The Jedi use "the Force" for good, and the Sith use its "Dark Side" for evil in an attempt to take over the galaxy. The first "trilogy" included *Star Wars* 1977 (later, *Episode IV: A New Hope*), *The Empire Strikes Back* (1980) and *Return of the Jedi* (1983). Two decades later, the series continued with a prequel trilogy; *Episode I: The Phantom Menace* (1999), *Episode II: Attack of the Clones* (2002), and *Episode III: Revenge of the Sith* (2005). Since then, George Lucas sold the rights to Disney (2012) for a little over $4 billion according to Matt Krantz in *USA Today. Star Wars: The Force Awakens* (Episode

VII) is scheduled for release in December 2015. Episodes VIII and IX are planned for 2017 and 2019 respectively.

Many have tried to articulate what sparked the magnetism of the earliest Star Wars Trilogy, especially the first film entitled simply *Star Wars*. In an interview between George Lucas and Bill Moyers in 1999 entitled *The Mythology of Star Wars*, Lucas sheds some light on that mystery and acknowledges his debt to Joseph Campbell, well-known expert in world mythology, and author of many books on the subject. Campbell's *Hero with a Thousand Faces* (1949) is a study of the hero myth, a universal pattern that is the essence of and common to, heroic tales in every culture. The Mythic Hero journeys outward, away from the "world" as he knows it. However, he soon realizes he is on a Quest in search of something larger than himself. In order to find it, he must leave behind his old life, endure great hardship, and embrace a new way of living. (Sounds a lot like Abraham's journey, doesn't it?)

The whole idea of the Mythic Hero's Journey resonates with each of us as we journey through life, Campbell maintains, but added in a famous PBS special entitled *The Power of Myth*, that "the process takes time." In today's world, he said (and this was in the late 1988), changes occur so quickly we often don't see such a "journey" as possible. Perhaps this is why the *Star Wars* epic had such resonance in 1977 and continues to do so almost forty years later: it slows down the process of the Heroic Journey and suggests that in a time when changes occur at an exponential rate, the journey may take generations to complete.

George Lucas knew Joseph Campbell personally and considered him a mentor, especially in his crafting of the *Star Wars* saga. In his 1999 interview with Bill Moyers, Lucas claims to believe, as Campbell did, that myths are stories that come from the natural world and reveal to us clues about our sacred nature. He claims that in *Star Wars* he sought to "recreate myth and mythic motifs" to deal with "today's issues," to "tell old myths in a new way." One epic theme with which Lucas sought to deal, he acknowledges, is the interconnectedness of all things. Another is redemption. Darth Vader is redeemed by his children, Lucas says. "It's what life's about." Children are the best part of life and we have to "let go of the past and embrace the future." In the end, Lucas maintains that what is important is "how you conduct yourself as you go through life." Each of us has our own "hero's journey" that Lucas hopes will lead us to "put the welfare of the community above the self." "All of us teach everyday of our lives," Lucas says at the end of the interview, suggesting that his impetus for selling the Star Wars franchise to Disney thirteen years later may be two-fold: to teach and keep the myth alive for the next generation.

Conclusion

In a few short pages, we have sampled some of the "Stories that Changed the World." We began our search far back into our species' Ice Age beginnings some 100,000 years ago. It's a fascinating beginning to our Human Story. A period of glaciation waxed and waned over 2.6 million years, the last such period peaking about 22,000 years ago and ending about 11,500 years ago. During this time, *Homo sapiens* evolved while many large mammals (wooly mammoths, saber-toothed tigers, giant ground sloths, and his closest human competitors) became extinct.

And we have investigated the role that storytelling has played in our journey across the planet. Storytelling is a significant factor in our "human-ness" and our ability to dominate the Earth. No other species has done this. As far as we know, no other species is self-aware, endowed with a consciousness as are we, *Homo sapiens*. And with the recent scientific research into the workings of our brains, we are beginning to understand why our storytelling abilities have played such an integral role for our species and to anticipate the role these abilities may play in the future stories we tell.

Three books have influenced my understanding of storytelling's importance. The first I encountered in graduate school at Rice University: Raymond Williams' *Marxism and Literature* (1977). This dense work of literary criticism introduced me to the concept of a literary time-line going back into the past toward prehistory and forward toward a future that had yet to unfold. Along the timeline were storytellers who had taken from past human experience and left their own "products" (stories) along the way. In Williams' sense, each author's stories were "products" of all works that came before them, and they in turn influenced all stories that came after.

The book *Finite and Infinite Games: A Vision of Life and Play and Possibility* (1986) by James P. Carse, now Professor Emeritus at New York University, was also influential. Toward the end of his book, Carse talks about the "choral nature" of history and the role of myth: "As myths make individual experience possible," he says, "they also make collective experience possible. Whole civilizations rise from stories—and can rise from nothing else" (141). In the book's final pages, he remarks on the importance of storytelling in an historical context. "Infinite players are not serious actors in any story, but the joyful poets of a story that continues to originate what they cannot finish." Exactly. Serious storytellers generate narratives that become building blocks of the larger narrative—the Human Narrative; any other storytelling endeavor will achieve only a finite end.

Many years ago, I finished my dissertation on Thomas Pynchon with Roger Penrose's *The Emperor's New Mind: Concerning Computers, Minds, and the Laws of Physics* (1989) in tatters from my efforts to tease from Pynchon's novels that tantalizing "space" between myth and science. Penrose proposed at the time that the "striking feature of inspirational thought is its 'global character.'" Arguing against the idea that a machine can achieve true Artificial Intelligence, he gave several examples of "inspirational thought" that seems to have occurred because of inspiration's "global nature" in the brain: August Kekule claimed to have "dreamed" the structure of the benzene molecule after countless months of bafflement; Henri Poincaré solved a difficult mathematical problem as he stepped onto a street car in a city where he was vacationing; Mozart *heard* his compositions finished in his head before he wrote them down.

Penrose's insights may seem prophetic to some, given recent research involving the brain's operations. His insights may seem naïve to others who believe that artificial intelligence is poised to become a reality before the century's end. Ray Kurzweil is one of those AI advocates; he asserts that the "singularity" (the moment when Artificial Intelligence overtakes human thinking) will be reached by 2029. Most AI proponents project the moment to be about forty-five years out but feel certain it will occur before the end of the century. Kurzweil may have some odd ideas, but he's been a successful technologist and entrepreneur and has invented dozens of devices that have changed our world (the flat-bed scanner, the first text-to-speech synthesizer). Kurzweil works for Google as its Director of Engineering and has assembled, according to Carol Cadwalladr in a 2014 article in *The Guardian*, "the greatest artificial intelligence laboratory on Earth." AI has been a dream of Google founders Larry Page and Sergey Brin since the start-up of Google, and Google-scale resources are beyond any data pool the world has ever seen. Google is buying up machine-learning and robotics companies at an amazing rate, including the British artificial intelligence startup DeepMind (£242 million). Other companies are chasing AI as well, but Google (Google X) has a definite lead.

According to O. B. Hardison, Jr. in his ambitious and prophetic book, *Disappearing through the Skylight* (1989), as long ago as 1983, William McLaughlin of the Cal Tech Jet Propulsion Laboratory argued, "the close of the 21st century should bring the end of human dominance of Earth." And as recently as December 2014, Stephen Hawking told the BBC that the "development of full artificial intelligence could spell the end of the human race." In a world actively seeking and may well develop "full artificial intelligence" in this century, what weapon does the average human being have to defend oneself?

Storytelling.

Storytelling through the humanities.

And if so, what kind of stories shall we tell?

In his recent book, *The Storytelling Animal: How Stories Make Us Human,* Jonathan Gottschall devotes a final chapter to "The Future of Story." In this chapter, he suggests that Massively Multiplayer Online Roleplaying Games (MMORPGs) like *World of Warcraft, Starwars: the Old Republic,* and *Runescape* most certainly will lead us toward stories of the future. With the active collective accounts of the three games mentioned totaling almost 30 million at the publication of his book (2014), it's hard not to give his idea serious consideration. Many "gamers," he says, form satisfying "in-game" friendships and believe the virtual world is "more authentically human than the real world"; online role playing games give players a sense of community, confidence, and an image for others to admire, Gottschall says. He seems optimistic that these gaming "stories" may eventually "outstrip real life" and become so addictive as to encourage a mass exodus from the real world into the virtual. But looked at from a perspective different from Gottschall's, one more in line with that of Carse in *Finite and Infinite Games,* MMORPG games seem like the antithesis of storytelling. The MMORPG player may begin to lose the conscious "self" and become instead a "player" in the virtual world imagined and created by game developers and designers who control that world. The very purpose of playing an MMORPG is *not* to "empathize" with the story's characters in order to enlarge one's experience, but to *annihilate* them in order to *assert oneself.* Role playing games have as their goal an endgame of victory and power. Winners live. Losers die. MMORPGs are, if anything, *anti-stories* in which millions of players on a global scale surrender their conscious selves, play for the privilege of being the last one standing in a world created, marketed, and controlled by developers and designers and the companies that hire them.

A broader, for more optimistic view the story's future comes once again from biologist Edward O. Wilson in *The Meaning of Human Existence.* Throughout his book, Wilson champions the role of the humanities in the future of human existence. Wilson maintains that "Conscious mental life . . . is a constant review of stories experienced in the past and competing stories invented for the future with the 'self' on center stage," an idea supported by research in neuroscience. Wilson declares that, even when the rate of scientific knowledge and technological advances slows (and he assures us it will), the humanities "will continue to evolve and diversity indefinitely". This is because the humanities constitute "the essence of the human character," he tells us; they are the "soul" of our species. Throughout our existence, the humanities—storytelling disciplines, all—have consistently empowered us to embrace our future with hope, encouraged us to conduct ourselves with dignity, inspired us to leave the human community better than we found it. Even when every storyteller does not have this as a goal, the humanities have enabled us to make our individual journeys heroic, not because we wish to be the last player standing, but because we choose to journey outward and participate in a story larger than our own. And now, as we face a future fraught with uncertainty and populated with technologies we are compelled to develop but unsure how to control, the humanities, if cultivated, can preserve and continue

Homo sapiens' most powerful legacy: An awareness that we are unique among all species, an understanding that our stories must endure.

Some stories will change our world.

Works Cited

Cadwalladr, Carole. "Are the Robots about to Rise?" *The Guardian*. 22 February 2014. Accessed 23 April 2015.

Cahill, Thomas. *The Gifts of the Jews: How a Tribe of Desert Nomads Changed the Way Everyone Thinks and Feels*. New York: Doubleday, 1998.

Campbell, Joseph with Bill Moyers. *The Power of Myth*. PBS. 1988. 25th Anniversary Edition. Athena. 2014.

Carse, James P. *Finite and Infinite Gamers: A Vision of Life as Play and Possibility*. New York: Macmillan, 1986.

"Furore over 'Censored' Edition of *Huckleberry Finn*." BBC News. http://www.bbc.com/news/world-us-canada-12126700 Accessed 27 May 2015.

Gazzaniga, Michael S., Richard B. Ivry, and George R. Mangun. *Cognitive Neuroscience: The Biology of the Mind*. 4th ed. New York: W. W. Norton, 2014.

Gots, Jason. "Your Storytelling Brain." Big Think. www.bigthink.com. n.d. Accessed 21 Jan. 2015.

Gottschall, Jonathan. *The Storytelling Animal: How Stories Make Us Human*. New York: Houghton Mifflin/Harcourt Publishing, 2012.

"Guernica: Testimony of War." PBS. *Treasures of the World*. http://www.pbs.org/treasuresoftheworld/a_nav/guernica_nav/main_guerfrm.html Accessed 26 May 2015.

Hardison, O. B. Jr. *Disappearing through the Skylight*. New York: Viking, 1989.

Hasson, Uri, et.al. "Brain-to-Brain Coupling: A Mechanism for Creating and Sharing a Social World. *Trends in Cognitive Sciences*. 16.2 (February 2012): 93-132.

Hitler, Adolf. *Mein Kampf*. The Ford Translation. 2nd Ed. Elite Minds, Inc. 2009-10.

Huxley, Aldous. "Propaganda under a Dictatorship." *Brave New World Revisited*. 1958. www.huxley.net/bnw-revisited/ Accessed 7 March 2015.

"Immigration Demographics in the U. S." http://www.sourcewatch.org/index.php/Immigration_demographics_in_the_U.S. Accessed 28 May 2015.

Krantz, Matt, et. Al. "Disney Buys Lucasfilm for $4 Billion." *USA Today*. 30 October 2012. http://www.usatoday.com/story/money/business/2012/10/30/disney-star-wars-lucasfilm/1669739/ Accessed 29 May 2015.

Moyers, Bill. *The Mythology of Star Wars*. Excerpted interview with George Lucas, 1999. *The Power Of Myth*. PBS. 25th Anniversary Edition. Athena, 2014.

NPR. "Igor Stravinsky's 'The Rite of Spring' with Thomas Kelly." *NPR's Performance Today: Milestones of the Millennium*. Lisa Simeone, host. 1999.

Nabben, Jenny. "The Science behind Storytelling." www.melcrum.com. n.d. Accessed 7 Mar. 2015.

Penrose, Roger. *The Emperor's New Mind: Concerning Computers, Minds, and the Laws of Physics*. New York: Penguin, 1989.

Rosefield, Jayne. "Wagner's Influence on Hitler and Hitler's on Wagner." From *History Review*. 1998. http://www.historytoday.com/jayne-rosefield/wagners-influence-hitler-and-hitlers-wagner. Accessed 22 May 2015.

Smithsonian. "Human Family Tree." http://humanorigins.si.edu/evidence/human-family-tree Accessed 3 February 2015.

"Stravinsky's *The Rite of Spring*." PBS. *Keeping Score*. http://www.pbs.org/keepingscore/stravinsky-rite-of-spring.html Accessed 31 May 2015.

Tattersall, Ian. "How We Came to be Human." *2006 Special Edition Scientific American: Becoming Human.* 66-73. Print.

Williams, Raymond. *Marxism and Literature.* New York. Oxford. 1977.

Wilson, Edward O. *The Meaning of Human Existence.* New York: W. W. Norton, 2014.

Zak, Paul J. "How Stories Change the Brain." *Greater Good.* http:// greatgood.berkeley.edu. 17 Dec. 2013. Accessed 21 Jan. 2014.